CIVIL WAR LETTERS

From Home, Camp & Battlefield

Edited by BOB BLAISDELL

DOVER PUBLICATIONS, INC.
Mineola, New York

Acknowledgments

Letter on page 133. APPROACH TO GETTYSBURG: **Iowa Michigan Royster,** C.S.A., to his mother (June 29, 1863). Used with permission from Southern Historical Collection, University of North Carolina, Chapel Hill. Copyright 2002 by the Rector and Visitors of the University of Virginia.

Bibliographical Note

Civil War Letters: From Home, Camp and Battlefield is a new work, first published by Dover Publications, Inc., in 2012. The black and white illustrations interspersed throughout the text have been selected from *An Artist's Story of the Great War, vol. I,* by Edwin Forbes, originally published by Fords, Howard & Hulbert, New York, in 1890.

Library of Congress Cataloging-in-Publication Data

Civil War letters: from home, camp and battlefield / edited by Bob Blaisdell.
   p. cm.
Includes bibliographical references.
ISBN-13: 978-0-486-48450-1
ISBN-10: 0-486-48450-5
1. United States—History—Civil War, 1861–1865—Sources. 2. United States—History—Civil War, 1861–1865—Personal narratives. 3. Soldiers—United States—Correspondence. 4. United States. Army—History—Civil War, 1861–1865—Sources. 5. Confederate States of America. Army—History—Sources. I. Blaisdell, Robert.
E464.C485 2012
973.7—dc23

                                                                2011029400

Manufactured in the United States by Courier Corporation
48450502   2013
www.doverpublications.com

A Dispatch Bearer

Contents

~ 1865 ~

Note

EACH OF THE ninety-four letters in this book represents a million more[1]. During the Civil War years 1861–1865, soldiers' letters home from camps, battlefields and hospitals could shine with rays of hope and glory when they were not bearing thunderbolts of tragedy. Letters *from* home, at the same time, animated and refocused those soldiers. Two years into the war, Union Captain Charles Francis Adams, Jr., wrote from Amissville, Virginia: "letters are more than ever before prized by me, for now they constitute absolutely my only link with the world and my own past, and moreover my only pleasure.... You should see the news fly round the camp and the men's faces light up, and how duty, discipline, everything, at once gives way to the reading of the letters. It's like fresh water in an August noon."

Though the soldiers and officers regularly discuss the joy of receiving letters, this collection puts us in the frame of mind of the

---

1 "While precise numbers are simply not available, we know that letters carried to and from the armies numbered in the tens of millions over the course of four years.... The military mail of the 1860s was unique in benefiting from a mass communications system that had not yet established a regular system of surveillance." Robert E. Bonner. *The Soldier's Pen: Firsthand Impressions of the Civil War.* New York: Hill and Wang, 2006.

families and friends anticipating dreadful news, which was always on the verge of arriving. We see that these warriors, however, *need* to communicate the occupation of their minds, the terrors they witness, the boredom they suffer, the spirit that animates the faith in their cause, their realizations of gratitude and heartache. The act of composing letters drew amazed reflections from the authors. Confederate Private Thomas D. Newton confesses to his sister: "This evening, the 20th of May, affords me the delightful pleasure of writing to you all at home. Home. Home. How much pleasure there is in that word home? There is more than tongue can express. How oft have I thought of home. That place that I formerly so little appreciated. And to think of those that are there. The kind Father, the indulgent Mother to which I have been so disrespectful in days gone by. The fond sisters that I have so oft mistreated. Oh, that I could have my time over again how different I would live."

While many of the writers here are the great and renowned, many are simply among the hundreds of thousands who enlisted. This collection favors personal over official letters, as the letter writers have no alternative but to be themselves, the human beings their friends and families know, miss and love. The men are conscious of being read; they sometimes spare their loved ones the gruesome details; sometimes, those details snake through anyway and expose the dread haunting the combatants. The young men irrepressibly show their humanity, their weariness and unhappiness, their Christian resignation and resolve as well as their family bonds. There are in fact also several letters of official business, including the note from Major Robert Anderson refusing to evacuate his troops from Fort Sumter and the consequent Confederate bombardment that commenced the four years of violence; Robert E. Lee's agonized offer to Jefferson Davis to resign after his defeat at Gettysburg; William Tecumseh Sherman's exultant announcement in 1864 of his Christmas "gift" of Savannah to President Lincoln; and finally Ulysses S. Grant's letter on April 9, 1865, setting the terms of surrender of Lee's Army of Northern Virginia.

I have arranged the letters by date, even if by doing so it interrupts a sequence between correspondents. I have identified writers with their "affiliation," Confederate (C.S.A.) or Union (U.S.A.). While literacy was pervasive in mid-nineteenth century America, correct spelling and grammar were not; I have modernized spellings, usually, and spelled out many abbreviations. I have added punctuation and paragraph breaks for clarity. Most of the letters are complete, but some are excerpts, notably Stonewall Jackson's, whose wife in her memoirs clipped his extraordinary effusions. I have headed each letter with a title referencing a place, battle or subject, and selected a quotation to further identify the topic or highlight. (The lettered code following each selection is keyed to the list of Sources on page 205.) The attempt to suggest the variety of the personalities and stories that animate our knowledge of the war will, I hope, lead readers to discover the treasure troves of letters by the famous men and women of the time as well as the correspondence by the everyday soldiers and families that are still generously being made available by university and public libraries.

—Bob Blaisdell
New York City
June 20, 2011

1861

FORT SUMTER: *"your communication, demanding the evacuation of this Fort"*

Major Robert Anderson, U.S.A.
Fort Sumter, South Carolina
April 11, 1861

To General P. G. T. Beauregard, C.S.A.

Sir:—

I have the honor to acknowledge receipt of your communication, demanding the evacuation of this Fort, and to say in reply thereto that it is a demand with which I regret that my sense of honor and my obligations to my Government prevent my compliance.

Source: The Union Reader, etc. [UR]

The next afternoon at 3:30, Beauregard's aides-de-camp delivered this reply: "By virtue of Brigadier General Beauregard's command, we have the honor to notify you that he will open the line of his batteries on Fort Sumter in one hour from this time." And so came the shots that started the war.

~

RESIGNING FROM THE UNITED STATES ARMY: *"Save in defense of my native State, I never desire again to draw my sword"*

Colonel Robert E. Lee, U.S.A.
First Cavalry
Arlington, Virginia
April 20, 1861

To General Winfield Scott, U.S.A.

General:

Since my interview with you on the 18th inst. I have felt that I ought no longer to retain my commission in the Army. I therefore tender my resignation, which I request you will recommend for acceptance. It would have been presented at once but for the struggle it has cost me to separate myself from a service to which I have devoted all the best years of my life and all the ability I possessed.

During the whole of that time—more than a quarter of a century—I have experienced nothing but kindness from my superiors, and the most cordial friendship from my comrades. To no one, General, have I been as much indebted as to yourself for uniform kindness and consideration, and it has always been my ardent desire to meet your approbation. I shall carry to the grave the most grateful recollections of your kind consideration, and your name and fame will always be dear to me.

Save in defense of my native State, I never desire again to draw my sword. Be pleased to accept my most earnest wishes for the continuance of your happiness and prosperity, and believe me,

Most truly yours,
R. E. LEE

After Virginia's secession from the Union on April 17, Lee (1807–1870) turned down the offer from General Scott and President Lincoln to become the commander of the United States Army. He became

the Confederacy's most important general and by the war's end was the army's commander in chief.

Source: [REL]

~

BATTLE OF BIG BETHEL: *"It was a strange sensation standing there, awaiting the approach of the foe for the first time"*

Private Alfred Davenport, U.S.A.
Fifth Regiment, New York State Duryee Zouaves
Camp Butler, Fortress Monroe, Virginia
June 11, 1861

To His Mother

I suppose that ere this you have heard of our engagement with the enemy. Sunday evening we were out on parade as usual. After we were dismissed we were called together again, and each man given twenty rounds of ammunition, in addition to what we already had. All was bustle and activity: we knew we were going somewhere, but as to the direction we were completely in the dark. Taps were sounded as usual, and we were ordered to our tents. A few minutes after a man might be seen going to each tent, and whispering the words, "At half-past ten every man will be called; he will immediately, and without noise or light, arise, equip himself, and fall in line in front of the tents. He will be supplied with one day's rations; will also tie his turban around his left arm twice, as a distinguishing mark."

About an hour before the time I was outside of my tent, when I saw a body of men going by: they made so little noise that it seemed to me mysterious where they had come from. I learnt that they were two of our companies, who were to go ahead as skirmishers under the command of Captains Kilpatrick (now major-general of cavalry) and Bartlett. I now understood that we were to surprise a rebel camp about fifteen miles from here. It seems that a negro who had ran away from the rebels, being employed by them to help build their batteries, had given information of it, which led General Butler to determine to attack it. There were several secessionists who came down to Hampton for the purpose of shooting the negro. We were to act in conjunction with a regiment at Newport News, and others were to follow us.

We were finally on the march. Nobody would have thought that a large body of men were on the move, by the stillness that prevailed. After we had gone some five or six miles, we were ordered to halt. I looked through the woods and saw a bright light; it could not be mistaken, it was a rebel signal: it was in a house, and pointed directly in the line of their company. Further on we came in sight of another. Soon after we came to a slight halt, heard a volley of musketry, and were ordered on at a double-quick. Our company being on the right was ahead of the line, and I am near the head, so that I had a chance to see everything. We halted, and found that we had come upon the extreme outpost. There was a campfire burning, and we had taken an officer prisoner. He was well mounted, with a fine revolver and sword, the edge of which was sharpened up to the handle. He was a fine looking man, over six feet high. We then heard rapid firing in the rear. We supposed that the rebels had come in contact with the Newport News regiment under Colonel Bendix. We soon saw that a most lamentable mistake had occurred. Colonel Bendix in the uncertain light of morning had taken Colonel Townsend's 3rd N.Y. regiment, who were following after us, for an enemy, and engaged them! The result was that eleven were wounded, some probably mortally!

Our commander now determined to go back and attack the camp. We started, but not before we had burned down a very handsome, well-furnished house, from which one of our men had been shot dead. Further on we burned down a low wooden hut, known as the "Little Bethel," a noted place of meeting for spies and secret orders.

We finally came upon the enemy, tired and exhausted. We learned from negroes that they were very strong and had more men than we had. We were so close to their batteries that we could hear them calling "Turn out!" "Turn out!" and the drums beating the "long roll."

Captain Kilpatrick threw out his skirmishers. We ascertained that there was a strong battery commanding the road, besides others to the left and right. It was a strange sensation standing there, awaiting the approach of the foe for the first time, expecting every moment to receive a volley from the woods into our closed ranks; but every man was firm: to be sure we looked a *shade* paler, but there was but one look, "to do or die."

Our captain said the ball had commenced. Instantaneously another report was heard, and a shell came whizzing through the air: now they came thick and fast.

We were ordered to charge through the wood. On we rushed through the brush, which was raked by grape and canister, bombs and rifled cannon. All the companies got mixed up in squads, and every man was his own officer. It now became too hot; we were obliged to get behind trees and stumps. Some of the boys crept close to a fence nearest the enemy, on the outskirts of the woods, and took advantage of every opportunity to pick off a man. Captain Kilpatrick was shot twice in the legs: he did not seem to mind it, but said, "It won't do to stay here and be shot down without doing any thing." He ordered the men to keep covered as well as they could and to *form*, but the brush was so thick that it was impossible to find captains, or any officers, or companies. Finally some few of us rushed out of the woods and across the road, headed by Lieutenant Jacob Duryea, a son of the colonel, and Captain Kilpatrick, notwithstanding his wounds, who is the most dashing officer in the regiment, and charged across a ploughed field with no cover after leaving the wood. In this charge there were not more than forty, and *all had red breeches*. We laid down often to escape shot. About the same time Colonel Townsend charged further to the left. The colonel was mounted, and sat on his white horse at the head of his men without flinching. We finally got to the cover of two old sheds, and were about four hundred feet from their batteries. We kept up fire for a short time, but it was folly to stay there any longer, as we were not supported. There was no concert of action or anybody to command, and

Drawing Their Fire.

most of the troops were lying behind stone walls, at a good distance to the rear. There were only three officers to be seen on that part of the field. I guess they did not like the fun. *Outside* of their fortifications we fear the rebels in no *way, shape, or manner.* General Price thought that the place could not be taken by storm without too much sacrifice of men.

The hardest part was held by the regulars' battery; they deserve the greatest credit and glory for holding their position on the road in such a raking fire. Lieutenant Greble was killed. The guns would have been spiked and left in the road, but our Colonel Warren, who appeared to be the only officer who knew what he was about, saved the guns, and, if he had had the command, would have taken the batteries. Captain Kilpatrick's company are also deserving of great credit for skirmishing duty.

Major Winthrop, aid to General Butler, and a very superior man, was picked off early by a sharp-shooter. He was showing himself carelessly while reconnoitring their position, and hence his death. Hoping that Providence will prosper our cause and give us the victory, I now close.

YOUR AFFECTIONATE SON

After the war, Davenport wrote Camp and Field Life of the Fifth New York Volunteer Infantry *(1879).*

Source: [SL]

~

BATTLE OF FALLING WATERS: *"My officers and men behaved beautifully, and were anxious for a battle, this being only a skirmish"*

Colonel Thomas J. (Stonewall) Jackson, C.S.A.
First Brigade, Army of the Shenandoah
July 4, 1861

To His Wife, Mary Anna Jackson

My precious darling, day before yesterday I learned that the enemy had crossed the Potomac and were advancing upon me. I immediately ordered my command under arms, and gave such instructions as I desired to have carried out until I should be heard from again, and with Captain Pendleton's Battery and one regiment of Virginia volunteers advanced to meet the Federal troops. After proceeding to the locality which had been indicated as occupied by them, and ascertaining the position of their advance, I made the necessary movement for bringing a small part of my force into action. Soon the firing commenced, and the advance of the enemy was driven back. They again advanced, and were repulsed. My men got possession of a house and barn, which gave them a covered position and an effective fire; but finding that the enemy were endeavoring to get in my rear and that my men were being endangered, I gave the order to their colonel that, if pressed, he must fall back. He obeyed, and fell back. The artillery of the foe opened upon me, and I directed Captain Pendleton to take a favorable position in rear and return their fire with one gun. His first ball cleared the road, which was occupied by the enemy.

I still continued to fall back, checking the enemy when it became necessary, so as to give time for my baggage to get into column at camp before I should arrive there, as one of my objects in advancing was to keep the enemy from reaching my camp before my wagons could get out of the way. Besides my cavalry, I had only one regiment engaged, and one cannon, though I had ordered up two other regiments, so as to use them if necessary. My cannon fired only eight times, while the enemy fired about thirty-five times; but the first fire of Captain Pendleton's Battery was probably worth more than all of theirs. I desired, as far as practicable, to save my ammunition. My orders from General Johnston required me to retreat in the event of the advance in force of the enemy, so as soon as I ascertained that he was in force I obeyed my instructions. I had twelve wounded and thirteen killed and missing. My cavalry took forty-nine prisoners. A number of the enemy were killed, but I do not know how many. As I obeyed my orders, and fell back, after ascertaining that the Federals were in force, the killed of the enemy did not fall into our hands. My officers and men behaved beautifully, and were anxious for a battle, this being only a skirmish. I wrote out my official report last night, and think General Johnston forwarded it to Richmond.

This morning one of his staff-officers told me that the general had recommended me for a brigadier-general. I am very thankful that an ever-kind Providence made me an instrument in carrying out General Johnston's orders so successfully.... The enemy are celebrating the 4th of July in Martinsburg, but we are not observing the day.

Jackson (1824–1863) was among the most charismatic and successful of the war's generals. (He earned his nickname "Stonewall" at the First Battle of Manassas. See the letter of July 22, 1861, below.) His widow noted of this letter: "It is said that, before firing this first ball upon the enemy, the reverend officer lifted his eyes to heaven and uttered the prayer, 'Lord, have mercy upon their souls!'"

Source: [MSJ]

∼

Major Sullivan Ballou, U.S.A.
Second Regiment, Rhode Island Volunteers
Washington, D.C.
July 14, 1861

My Very Dear Wife:

The indications are very strong that we shall move in a few days, perhaps tomorrow. Lest I should not be able to write you again, I feel impelled to write a few lines, that may fall under your eye when I shall be no more.

Our movement may be one of a few days duration and full of pleasure—and it may be one of severe conflict and death to me. Not my will, but thine, O God, be done. If it is necessary that I should fall on the battle-field for my country, I am ready. I have no misgivings about, or lack of confidence in, the cause in which I am engaged, and my courage does not halt or falter. I know how strongly American civilization now leans upon the triumph of the government, and how great a debt we owe to those who went before us through the blood and suffering of the Revolution, and I am willing, perfectly willing to lay down all my joys in this life to help maintain this government, and to pay that debt.

But, my dear wife, when I know, that, with my own joys, I lay down nearly all of yours, and replace them in this life with cares and sorrows,—when, after having eaten for long years the bitter fruit of orphanage myself, I must offer it, as their only sustenance, to my dear little children, is it weak or dishonorable, while the banner of my purpose floats calmly and proudly in the breeze, that my unbounded love for you, my darling wife and children, should struggle in fierce, though useless, contest with my love of country.

I cannot describe to you my feelings on this calm summer night, when two thousand men are sleeping around me, many of them enjoying the last, perhaps, before that of death,—and I, suspicious that Death is creeping behind me with his fatal dart, am communing with God, my country and thee.

I have sought most closely and diligently, and often in my breast, for a wrong motive in thus hazarding the happiness of those I loved, and I could not find one. A pure love of my country, and of the principles I have often advocated before the people, and "the name of honor, that I love more than I fear death," have called upon me, and I have obeyed.

Sarah, my love for you is deathless. It seems to bind me with mighty cables, that nothing but Omnipotence can break; and yet, my love of country comes over me like a strong wind, and bears me irresistibly on with all those chains, to the battlefield. The memories of all the blissful moments I have spent with you, come crowding over me, and I feel most deeply grateful to God and you, that I have enjoyed them so long. And how hard it is for me to give them up, and burn to ashes the hopes of future years, when, God willing, we might still have lived and loved together, and seen our boys grow up to honorable manhood around us.

I know I have but few claims upon Divine Providence, but something whispers to me, perhaps it is the wafted prayer of my little Edgar, that I shall return to my loved ones unharmed. If I do not, my dear Sarah, never forget how much I love you, nor that, when my last breath escapes me on the battle-field, it will whisper your name.

Forgive my many faults, and the many pains I have caused you. How thoughtless, how foolish I have oftentimes been! How gladly would I wash out with my tears, every little spot upon your happiness, and struggle with all the misfortune of this world, to shield you and my children from harm. But I cannot. I must watch you from the spirit land and hover near you, while you buffet the storms with your precious little freight, and wait with sad patience till we meet to part no more.

But, O Sarah, if the dead can come back to this earth, and flit unseen around those they loved, I shall always be near you—in the garish day, and the darkest night—amidst your happiest scenes and gloomiest hours—always, always; and, if the soft breeze fans your cheek, it shall be my breath; or the cool air cools your throbbing temples, it shall be my spirit passing by.

Sarah, do not mourn me dead; think I am gone, and wait for me, for we shall meet again.

As for my little boys, they will grow as I have done, and never know a father's love and care. Little Willie is too young to remember me long, and my blue-eyed Edgar will keep my frolics with him among the dimmest memories of his childhood. Sarah, I have unlimited confidence in your maternal care, and your development of their characters. Tell my two mothers, I call God's blessing upon them. O Sarah, I wait for you there! Come to me, and lead thither my children.

SULLIVAN

Ballou was killed at Manassas on July 21.

Source: Brown University in the Civil War: A Memorial. Edited by Henry S. Burrage. Providence: Providence Press Company, 1868.

∾

GOD'S WILL: *"I am in the path of duty, and that no evil can come nigh me"*

Brigadier General Thomas J. (Stonewall) Jackson, C.S.A.
Winchester, Virginia
July 16, 1861

To His Wife, Mary Anna Jackson

...Last evening the enemy encamped at Bunker Hill, about ten miles from us, and this morning we would have given them a warm reception had they advanced, but we have heard nothing respecting their movements today. The news from the Northwest is unfavorable, as you have probably seen in the papers, but we must not be discouraged. God will, I am well satisfied, in His own good time and way, give us the victory....

In reply to your queries, I am sleeping on the floor of a good room, but I have been sleeping out in camp several weeks, and generally found that it agreed with me well, except when it rained, and even then it was but slightly objectionable. I find that sleeping in the open air, with no covering but my blankets and the blue sky for a canopy, is more refreshing than sleeping in a room. My table

is rather poor, but usually I get corn-bread. All things considered, however, I am doing well....

As to writing so as to mail letters which would travel on Sunday, when it can be avoided, I have never had occasion, after years of experience, to regret our system. Although sister I—— gets letters from her husband every day, is she any happier than my *esposita?* Look how our kind Heavenly Father has prospered us! I feel well assured that in following our rule, which is Biblical, I am in the path of duty, and that no evil can come nigh me. All things work together for my good. But when my sweet one writes, let the letters be long, and your *esposo* hopes to send you full ones in return; and when the wars and troubles are all over, I trust that, through divine mercy, we shall have many happy days together.

"He always wrote and talked in the same hopeful, cheerful strain, never seeming to entertain a thought that he might fall; or if he had such a thought, he was too unselfish to overshadow his wife's happiness by intimating it to her. With the apostle Paul, he could say that 'living or dying he was the Lord's,' but he never expressed a desire to live so

strongly as not to survive his wife. From the very thought of such a bereavement, his affectionate nature seemed to shrink and recoil more than from any earthly calamity, and he often expressed the hope, with the greatest fervor and tenderness, that whatever trial his Heavenly Father sent upon him, this might be spared. In sickness, he was the most devoted of nurses—his great and loving heart having not a fibre of selfishness in it, and there was no end to the self-sacrifice he would endure."—Mary Anna Jackson.

Source: [MSJ]

∽

ENLISTMENT: *"I could not but rejoice that I had a son to offer to the service of the country, and if I had a dozen,* I would most freely give them all"

Reverend Robert Ryland
President, Richmond College
Richmond, Virginia
July 17, 1861

My Dear Son,—

It may have seemed strange to you that a professing Christian father so freely gave you, a Christian son, to enlist in the volunteer service. My reason was that I regarded this as a *purely defensive war.* Not only did the Southern Confederacy propose to adjust the pending difficulties by peaceful and equitable negotiations, but Virginia used again and again the most earnest and noble efforts to prevent a resort to the sword. These overtures having been proudly spurned, and our beloved South having been threatened with invasion and subjugation, it seemed to me that nothing was left us but stern resistance, or abject submission, to unconstitutional power. A brave and generous people could not for a moment hesitate between such alternatives. A war in defense of our homes and firesides, of our wives and children, of all that makes life worth possessing, is the result. While I most deeply deplored the necessity for the sacrifice, I could not but rejoice that

I had a son to offer to the service of the country, and if I had a dozen, *I would most freely give them all.* As you are now cheerfully enduring the hardships of the camp, I know you will listen to a father's suggestions touching the duties of your new mode of life.

1. Take special care of your health. More soldiers die of disease than in battle. A thin piece of damp sponge in the crown of your hat during exposure to the hot sun, the use of thick shoes and a water-proof coat in rainy weather, the practice of drinking cold water when you are very warm as slowly as you sip hot tea, the thorough mastication of your food, the avoiding of damp tents and damp grounds during sleep, and frequent ablutions of your person are all the hints I can give you on this point. Should you need anything that I can supply, let me hear from you. I will do what I can to make you comfortable. After all, you must learn to endure hardness as a good soldier. Having never slept a single night in your whole life except in a pleasant bed, and never known a scarcity of good food, you doubtless find the ways of the camp rough; but never mind. The war, I trust, will soon be over, and then the remembrance of your hardships will sweeten the joy of peace.

2. The rules of war require prompt and unquestioning obedience. You may sometimes think the command arbitrary and the officer supercilious, but *it is yours to obey.* An undisciplined army is a curse to its friends and a derision to its foes. Give your whole influence, therefore, to the maintenance of lawful authority and of strict order. Let your superiors feel assured that whatever they entrust to *you* will be faithfully done. Composed of such soldiers, and led by skillful and brave commanders, our army, by the blessing of God, will never be defeated. It is, moreover, engaged in a holy cause, and must triumph.

3. Try to maintain your Christian profession among your comrades. I need not caution you against strong drink as useless and hurtful, nor against profanity, so common among soldiers. Both these practices you abhor. Aim to take at once a decided stand for God. If practicable have prayers regularly in your tent, or unite with your fellow disciples in prayer meetings in the camp. Should preaching be accessible, always be a hearer. Let the world know that you are a Christian. Read a chapter fn the

14

New Testament, which your mother gave you, every morning and evening, when you can, and engage in secret prayer to God for his holy Spirit to guide and sustain you. I would rather hear of your death than of the shipwreck of your faith and good conscience.

4. As you will come into habitual contact with men of every grade, make special associates only of those whose influence on your character is felt to be good. Some men love to tell extravagant stories, to indulge in vulgar wit, to exult in a swaggering carriage, to pride themselves on their coarse manners, to boast of their heroism, and to give utterance to feelings of revenge against the enemy. All this is injurious to young and impressible minds. If you admire such things, you will insensibly imitate them, and imitation will work gradual but certain detriment to your character. Other men are refined without being affected. They can relax into occasional pleasantries without violating modesty. They can be loyal to their government without indulging private hatred against her foes. They can be cool and brave in battle, and not be braggarts in the absence of danger. Above all, they can be humble, spiritual, and active Christians, and yet mingle in the stirring and perilous duties of soldier-life. Let these be your companions and models. You will thus return from the dangers of camp without a blemish on your name.

5. Should it be your lot to enter into an engagement with the enemy, lift up your heart in secret ejaculations to the ever-present and good Being, that He will protect you from sudden death, or if you fall, that He will receive your departing spirit, cleansed in the blood of Jesus, into His kingdom. It is better to trust in the Lord than to put confidence in princes. Commit your eternal interests, therefore, to the keeping of the Almighty Saviour. You should not, even in the hour of deadly conflict, cherish personal rage against the enemy, any more than an officer of the law hates the victim of the law. How often does a victorious army tenderly care for the dead and wounded of the vanquished. War is a tremendous scourge which Providence sometimes uses to chastise proud and wicked nations. Both parties must suffer, even though one may get the advantage. There is no occasion then for adding to the intrinsic evils of the system the odious feature of animosity to individuals. In the ranks of the foe are

thousands of plain men who do not understand the principles for which we are struggling. They are deceived by artful demagogues into a posture of hostility to those whom, knowing, they would love. It is against such men that you may perhaps be arrayed, and the laws of war do not forbid you to pity them even in the act of destroying them. It is the more important that we should exhibit a proper temper in this unfortunate contest, because many professed Christians and ministers of the gospel at the North are breathing out, in their very prayers and sermons, threatenings and slaughter against us. Oh! how painful that a gray-headed pastor should publicly exclaim, *"I would hang them as quick at I would shoot a mad dog!"*

6. Providence has placed you in the midst of thoughtless and unpardoned men. What a beautiful thing it would be if you could win some of them to the Saviour. Will you not try? You will have many opportunities of saying a word in season. The sick you may comfort, the wavering you may confirm, the backslidden you may reclaim, the weary and heavy laden you may point to Jesus for rest to the soul. It is not presumptuous for a young man kindly and meekly to commend the gospel to his brother soldiers. The hardest of them will not repel a gentle approach, made in private. And many of them would doubtless be glad to have the subject introduced to them. They desire to hear of Jesus, but they lack courage to inquire of his people. An unusually large proportion of pious men have entered the army, and I trust they will give a new complexion to military life. Let them search out each other, and establish a fraternity among all the worshipers of God. To interchange religious views and administer brotherly counsel will be mutually edifying. "He that watereth shall be watered also himself."

And now, as a soldier has but little leisure, I will not occupy you longer. Be assured that every morning and evening we remember you, at the family altar, to our Father in Heaven. We pray for "a speedy, just, and honorable peace," and for the safe return of all the volunteers to their loved homes. All the children speak often of "brother," and hear your letters read with intense interest. That God Almighty may be your shield and your exceeding great reward, is the constant prayer of your loving father.

Ryland's son joined the infantry. Ryland (1805–1899) retired as president of Richmond College in 1866.

Source: [JMJ]

~

FIRST BATTLE OF MANASSAS (BULL RUN): *"Lincoln has overthrown the government of our forefathers"*

Private Randolph Harrison McKim, C.S.A.
First Maryland Infantry
Piedmont Station, Virginia
Saturday, July 20, 1861

My Most Precious Mother:

Mr. Hall has just made his appearance and handed me your letter and dear Margie's. It grieved me to the quick to find that you are still in ignorance of my real position in Virginia now, and I confess I almost felt self-reproached when you said that you were perfectly satisfied with my promise not to join the Southern Army "without my father's consent." I recollect full well writing the letter, and that was the thing which has kept me back so long from following what I have felt my duty to my country. This made me change my mind about joining when I had almost made up my mind to it some time ago, and this made me resolve to use every effort to get home and try and get consent to do so. I would not now be in the army, and would be at home, I expect, if the condition of things in Baltimore had not rendered it pretty certain that I would be arrested because I went in arms to Harper's Ferry.

I say then in justification of my course that I could not get home safely to get advice, and I felt very hopeful that papa, as most other Union men in Baltimore, had changed his sentiments when he found that the government means to establish a despotism and call it by the sacred name of Union. I do not now believe, after learning that I am disappointed to a great extent in this expected change so far, that papa will not finally cease to support what he has

17

believed a free and righteous government, when he finds beyond contradiction that Lincoln has overthrown the government of our forefathers and abolished every principle of the Declaration of Independence.

My dear, dear mother, I could hardly restrain tears in the midst of all the confusion and bustle of the camp this morning when I read your letter with those renewed expressions of your tender love for me. Oh, I hope you will not think me unworthy of such a love. If I have erred, do be lenient to me, you and papa both, and do not disown your son for doing what he felt to be a holy duty to his country. Papa, if you place yourself in my position, with the profound conviction I have of the holiness and righteousness of this Cause, ask yourself whether you would not have unhesitatingly done what I have done. You have yourself, in my hearing, placed the duty of country first in this world's duties and second only to the duty I owe my God. How then am I reprehensible for obeying what my very heart of hearts told me was my country's call, when I had some hope that your will would not be at variance with it, and I was unable to find out whether it was or not?

I have suffered much in mind and still do suffer. At all events I am not actuated by selfish or cowardly motives. How easy it would have been to sit down at quiet Belvidere, preserving an inactivity which all my friends would have regarded as honorable, than at the possible loss of your parental love and care, and at the sacrifice of my comforts and the risk of my life, to do what I have done—enlist as a common soldier (i.e., a volunteer private) in the cause of liberty and right! Camp life is a hard life—I know by experience. Forced marches, scanty provisions sometimes, menial offices to perform, perfect discipline to submit to, are not attractive features to anyone. Then military life has little charm for me. I have no taste for it, and no ambition for military glory. But I am ready and willing to suffer all these hardships, and, when necessary, to lay my life upon the altar of my country's freedom.

I hope I do not seem to boast or to glorify myself in speaking thus, but if I know my own heart this is the truth, and God give me grace to be consistent with this profession. Do not, my precious mother, be too much alarmed and too anxious about me. I trust and hope that God will protect me from "the terror

Something to eat

by night" and "the destruction that wasteth at noon-day." I feel as if my life was to be spared. I hope yet to preach the Gospel of the Lord Jesus Christ; but, my dear mother, we are in God's hands, and He doth not willingly afflict or grieve the children of men. "He that dwelleth in the secret place of the most High shall abide under the shadow of the Almighty." He does all things well, and He will give you grace to bear this trial too. Farewell, dear mother and father, Telfair, Mary, and Margie. I am, in this life and the next,

Your fond and affectionate
RANDOLPH

McKim (1842–1920) decided against informing his mother that the First Battle of Manassas would begin the next day.

Source: [ASR]

∽

FIRST BATTLE OF MANASSAS (BULL RUN): *"Let others speak praise, not myself"*

Brigadier General Thomas J. (Stonewall) Jackson, C.S.A.
Manassas, Virginia
July 22, 1861

To His Wife, Mary Anna Jackson

My Precious Pet,—

Yesterday we fought a great battle and gained a great victory, for which all the glory is due to *God alone*. Although under a heavy fire for several continuous hours, I received only one wound, the breaking of the longest finger of my left hand; but the doctor says the finger can be saved. It was broken about midway between the hand and knuckle, the ball passing on the side next the forefinger. Had it struck the centre, I should have lost the finger. My horse was wounded, but not killed. Your coat got an ugly wound near the hip, but my servant, who is very handy, has so far repaired it that it doesn't show very much. My preservation was

An Old Campaigner.

ONE OF THE BUCKTAILS.

entirely due, as was the glorious victory, to our God, to whom be all the honor, praise, and glory. The battle was the hardest that I have ever been in, but not near so hot in its fire. I commanded in the centre more particularly, though one of my regiments extended to the right for some distance. There were other commanders on my right and left. Whilst great credit is due to other parts of our gallant army, God made my brigade more instrumental than any other in repulsing the main attack. This is for your information only.—Say nothing about it. Let others speak praise, not myself.

"Though he was so reticent of his own part in the battle, it was well known that his brigade saved the day, the credit of which was justly given to its commander. At one moment it seemed as if all was lost. The troops of South Carolina, commanded by General Bee, had been overwhelmed, and he rode up to Jackson in despair, exclaiming, 'They are beating us back!' 'Then,' said Jackson, 'we will give them the bayonet!' This cool reply showed the unconquered mind of one who never knew that he was beaten, and put fresh courage into the heart of him who was almost ready to acknowledge defeat; and, as he rode back to his command, he cried out to them to 'look at Jackson!' saying, 'There he stands like a stone wall! Rally behind the Virginians!' The cry and the example had its effect, and the broken ranks were reformed, and led to another charge, when their leader fell dead with his face to the foe. But with his last breath he had christened his companion in arms, in the baptism of fire, with the name that he was henceforth to bear, not only in the Southern army, but in history, of Stonewall Jackson, while the troops that followed him on that day counted it glory enough to bear on their colors the proud title of the 'Stonewall Brigade.'"
—Mary Anna Jackson.

Source: [MSJ]

∾

IMAGINING HOME: *"I lay in my tent the other morning… and pictured to myself the dear old place"*

Private Randolph Harrison McKim, C.S.A.
Fairfax, Virginia
August 3, 1861

To His Mother

Though I have written I think three times since the battle to assure you of my safety, yet the news which Mr. —— brings, that I am reported among the killed in Baltimore, makes me anxious to embrace this new and certain opportunity of setting your mind at rest on this score, especially as the report is current at the University and in Richmond, and you may suppose it occurred in some way since the fight, on picket duty for instance. You have no idea how I long to see you and dear old Belvidere again. I lay in my tent the other morning while the rain poured in torrents outside, and pictured to myself the dear old place with the damasks on the porch, so fragrant, and then I entered the door in imagination and saw you all seated at a comfortable breakfast-table while I was almost drenched and obliged to fly to my crowded tent before completing my breakfast by half.

You should see me engaged in cooking, making fires, washing, etc. It is truly hard work and young men like Duncan, Wilson Carr and myself find that it is a difficult thing to make bread and coffee good enough to support life. Our mess consists of ten… We have no yeast, and so our bread must needs be heavy and indigestible as we have no means of rolling it out into biscuits. We make rice cakes though, and frequently get corn meal and make first-rate corn bread. We are able occasionally to get our bread cooked by the country people and we buy sometimes eggs, with a stray chicken or two. You have no idea how one gets accustomed to any sort of fare. I can now eat salt junk of the very fattest with great gusto, and drink coffee without milk, made in the company pot, and feel refreshed. The first hard washing of my clothes which I did, burned off the skin from my arms dreadfully.

Sometimes we have been out all day and part of the night in a drenching rain. In that forced march from Winchester to

Manassas we knew no distinction between night and day, but marched during both without rest almost, and almost entirely without food. Our regiment marches very fast and finds it very tiresome marching behind some Virginia and Tennessee regiments. We passed through Millwood, and Aunt Jane had her house lit up and was giving supper to all the soldiers who came in on their way. From five to six o'clock in the afternoon till three in the morning she was cooking for them, till she was eaten out of house and home nearly. We forded the Shenandoah up to our breasts and then marched on to Piedmont where we were delayed some time. We reached the Manassas Junction at 10:30 o'clock Sunday morning. As I told you, during the whole march we had not a single regular meal. Immediately after the victory we were marched back to Manassas (some six miles) and stayed there all Monday in a drenching rain, without tents, blankets or overcoats. Our company was out on picket duty night before last and we could hear the drums beating in the enemy's camp nearly all night long. We were within seven miles of Alexandria.

You would like to know how I spend a day here. The bugle sounds at half past four and then we go out to drill till six. Then we get breakfast, wash and get ready for drill again at nine o'clock. Then we drill an hour and a half or two hours. Then sleep, or write a letter, or clean up camp, or wash clothes, or put the tents

The Mud March.

in order. Then get dinner ready—drill again in the evening (the whole regiment together, battalion drill) at five o'clock. Dress parade at 6:30 p.m. Then supper. Soon after, at nine o'clock, the tattoo sounds and roll is called; then at 9:30 come three taps on the drum and all lights must instantly be extinguished. I have been very sick all day for the first time, but am nearly well now.

Good-by, my dear mother.—God bless and keep you all. I am sad often thinking of my dear home and longing to hear from you. Wish I could see you again just for one little day or week.

Never cease to pray for your fond son.

Source: [ASR]

~

PREPARING THE SOUTH FOR WAR: *"How thankless and ungrateful we are, and how we labor to mar His gifts"*

Brigadier General Robert E. Lee, C.S.A.
Huntersville, Pocahontas County, Virginia
August 4, 1861

To His Wife, Mary Lee

I reached here yesterday, dearest Mary, to visit this portion of the army. The day after my arrival at Staunton, I set off for Monterey, where the army of General Garnett's command is stationed. Two regiments and a field-battery occupy the Alleghany Mountains in advance, about thirty miles, and this division guards the road to Staunton. The division here guards the road leading by the Warm Springs to Milboro and Covington. Two regiments are advanced about twenty-eight miles to Middle Mountain. Fitzhugh [Major Fitzhugh Lee—General Lee's nephew] with his squadron is between that point and this. I have not seen him. I understand he is well. South of here again is another column of our enemies, making their way up the Kanawha Valley, and, from General Wise's report, are not far from Lewisburgh. Their object seems to be to get possession of the Virginia Central Railroad and the

Virginia and Tennessee Railroad. By the first they can approach Richmond; by the last interrupt our reinforcements from the South. The points from which we can be attacked are numerous, and their means are unlimited. So we must always be on the alert. My uneasiness on these points brought me out here.

It is so difficult to get our people, unaccustomed to the necessities of war, to comprehend and promptly execute the measures required for the occasion. . . .

The soldiers everywhere are sick. The measles are prevalent throughout the whole army, and you know that disease leaves unpleasant results, attacks on the lungs, typhoid, etc., especially in camp, where accommodations for the sick are poor.

I traveled from Staunton on horseback. A part of the road, as far as Buffalo Gap, I passed over in the summer of 1840, on my return to St. Louis, after bringing you home. If any one had then told me that the next time I traveled that road would have been on my present errand, I should have supposed him insane. I enjoyed the mountains, as I rode along. The views are magnificent—the valleys so beautiful, the scenery so peaceful. What a glorious world Almighty God has given us. How thankless and ungrateful we

Out of the Fight.

are, and how we labor to mar His gifts. I hope you received my
letters from Richmond. Give love to daughter and Mildred. I did
not see Rob [a son] as I passed through Charlottesville. He was at
the University and I could not stop.

Source: [REL]

~

SUFFERING FOOLS: *"I... only wish to save my country, and find the
incapables around me will not permit it!"*

Major General George B. McClellan, U.S.A.
Commander, Army of the Potomac
August 16, 1861, 1 a.m.

To Mary Ellen McClellan, His Wife

...I am here in a terrible place: the enemy have from three to
four times my force—the President is an idiot, the old general is
in his dotage—they cannot or will not see the true state of affairs.
Most of my troops are demoralized by the defeat at Bull Run;
some regiments even mutinous. I have probably stopped that; but
you see my position is not pleasant....

I have, I believe, made the best possible disposition of the few
men under my command; will quietly await events, and, if the
enemy attacks, will try to make my movements as rapid and
desperate as may be. If my men will only fight I think I can thrash
him, notwithstanding the disparity of numbers. As it is, I trust
to God to give success to our arms, though He is not wont to aid
those who refuse to aid themselves....

I am weary of all this. I have no ambition in the present affairs;
only wish to save my country, and find the incapables around
me will not permit it! They sit on the verge of the precipice,
and cannot realize what they see. Their reply to everything is,
"Impossible! Impossible!" They think nothing possible which is
against their wishes.

6 p.m.—...Gen. Scott is at last opening his eyes to the fact that I
am right and that we are in imminent danger. Providence is aiding

me by heavy rains, which are swelling the Potomac, which may be impassable for a week; if so we are saved. If Beauregard comes down upon us soon I have everything ready to make a maneuver which will be decisive. Give me two weeks and I will defy Beauregard; in a week the chances will be at least even.

George B. McClellan (1826–1885) was a West Point graduate and a highly regarded engineer. Ceaselessly full of himself, he became commander-in-chief of the Army in the fall of 1861. Two sources are cited for this letter, because in McClellan's memoirs he deleted some of the more grandiose claims for himself and the especially disparaging remarks concerning Lincoln and Scott.

Sources: [MOS] [GBM]

$\sim$

IN THE WEST: *"having truth and justice on our side, whilst on the other they are cheered on by falsehood and deception"*

Brigadier General Ulysses S. Grant, U.S.A.
Cairo, Illinois
September 11, 1861

To Mary Grant

Dear Sister:

Your letter with a short one from Father was received yesterday, and having a little time I answer it.

The troops under me and the rebel forces are getting so close together however that I have to watch all points. Since taking command I have taken possession of the Kentucky bank opposite here, fortified it and placed four large pieces in position. Have occupied Norfolk, Missouri, and taken possession of Paducah. My troops are so close to the enemy as to occasionally exchange shots with the pickets. Today, or rather last night, sixty or seventy rebels came upon seventeen of our men and were repulsed with a loss of two men killed on their side, none hurt on ours. Yesterday there was skirmishing all day. We had but two wounded however, whilst the loss must have been considerable on the other.

What future operations will be, of course I don't know. I could not write about it in advance if I did. The rebel force numerically is much stronger than ours, but the difference is more than made up by having truth and justice on our side, whilst on the other they are cheered on by falsehood and deception. This war however is formidable and I regret to say cannot end so soon as I anticipated at first....

My duties are very laborious and have been from the start. It is a rare thing that I get to bed before two or three o'clock in the morning and am usually wakened in the morning before getting awake in a natural way. Now, however, my staff are getting a little in the way of this kind of business and can help me.

I have been stopped so often already in writing this that I have forgotten what I was going to write about.

Are you talking of paying Julia [Grant's wife] a visit? I wrote to you and father about it several times but have failed to elicit an answer on that point. I intended to have Julia, Miss and Jess come down here to pay me a visit but I hardly think it would be prudent at this time.

Hearing artillery within a few miles it might embarrass my movements to have them about. I am afraid they would make poor soldiers.

Write to me again soon.

Good night.

ULYS

At the start of the war, the West Point graduate, a veteran of the Mexican War (1846–1848), was clerking in his father's leather store. He quickly proved his mettle as a military leader; he became the General in Chief of the Union Army in 1864.

Source: [USG]

⌒

Lieutenant Richard C. Derby, U.S.A.
15th Regiment, Massachusetts Volunteers
Poolesville, Maryland
October 22, 1861

To Reverend James Means

The news of the fight created great excitement in Worcester County, and many more people came on here than could be accommodated; but nobody blamed them for their anxiety, although they were really in the way. There happened to be unusual hospital accommodations, and all the wounded who were brought across the river received the best of care. Miss Dix has been up from Washington, and ordered a liberal supply of comforts. The wounds are all from gun-shots; and although dreadful to look at, only a small proportion are mortal. The weather is favorable for their healing. The fight was pronounced by all to have been a very severe one, and the ratio of loss was greater than at Bull Run. It is a mystery to me how *any man* escaped the shower of bullets that was poured in upon us for *two hours*. The pieces of artillery seemed to be the especial target of the sharp-shooters, and hardly a man was left standing by them after the second volley. I had always been afraid that the men would become unmanageable; but I was never more disappointed. Through the whole affair, from our embarkation in the miserable little skiffs to the retreat down the bluffs, they obeyed every order as promptly as though they were merely drilling, and fought as coolly as veterans. They showed the real English "pluck," and I think, if they had not seen that it was a hopeless and desperate fight, they would have added some of the French "dash," and carried everything before them.

Early in the forenoon, Co. H had a skirmish on its own account with a company of Mississippi riflemen. We got the better of them, even with our old smooth-bore muskets, but had to fall back to the shelter of the woods on the approach of cavalry. Our loss was seventeen killed and wounded in that affair, and

the same in the general battle. I went through the whole of it
without a scratch, not even a hole in my clothes. I was very much
disappointed, as some officers had three or four bullets through
their coats and caps: so I made up for it by nearly drowning myself
in the Potomac. I hadn't a suspicion but what I could swim across
with ease, so I pulled off my boots, and laid my sword, pistol,
and belt on a small board to push across. I was anxious to save
my sword, as it looked too much like surrendering to lose that.
I kept all my clothes on and my pockets full. I pushed off quite
deliberately, although the water was full of drowning soldiers
and bullets from the rebels on the top of the bluff. I made slow
progress with one hand, and had to abandon my raft and cargo.
I got along very well a little more than half way, when I found
that every effort I made only pushed my head under water, and it
suddenly flashed across me that I should drown. I didn't feel any
pain or exhaustion,—the sensation was exactly like being overcome
with drowsiness. I swallowed water in spite of all I could do, till at
last I sank unconscious.

There was a small island near Hartison's, against which the
current drifted me, and aroused me enough to crawl a step or two,
but not enough to know what I was doing till I dropped just at the
edge of the water with my head in the soft clay-mud. My good

fortune still continued, and Colonel Devens, swimming across on a log, landed right where I laid. He had me taken up and carried over to Harrison's Island to a good fire, where I soon began to feel quite comfortable, but was afterwards taken sick, and have been till this time recovering. I should have returned to duty today, if the weather hadn't been so stormy. I feel as if it was in answer to the many prayers of my friends that I was saved at last through so many dangers.

See also Derby's letter of December 15, 1861, below. Derby was one of 23,000 casualties at the battle of Antietam, September 17, 1862, where he died.

Source: [YC]

∾

GOD IN CAMP: *"Dear and Dearest wife, you wanted to know if I was trying to get religion or not"*

Private Henry H. Dedrick, C.S.A.
Allegany Mountain, Camp Tip Top
Pocahontas County, Virginia
December 9, 1861

To Mary E. A. Dedrick
Dear Wife—

It is with pleasure that I take my pen in hand to inform you that I am well at present. But I have had the mumps for better than a week. They did not hurt me much. I kept myself close and I hope when these few lines comes to hand that they may find you and the little boy enjoying good health and all the rest of my friends.

Dear Lissa, I received your most affectionate letter that you wrote on the fifth and the sixth on the eighth and I was truly glad to hear from you and to hear that you all was well and doing well. Dear wife, you wrote to me that you wanted to know if I had received the letter that you wrote to me the 22nd or not. I received the letter that you wrote on the 21st, the next day after I wrote that letter that Mr. Lewis brought you, and I answered it the 1st or the 2nd of this month. I thought that I would wait a few days as I had sent one by him and I had wrote one on the 5th to send it by Mr. L. Falls. He was coming to Staunton to bring some horses in and then he was coming home to see them all, but as other orders come he did not get to come and he returned it to me today. I get to see him and David Kennedy nearly every day, and James Trusler. They are all well at this time. James Trusler is working with Grass in the blacksmith shop. All the rest of the creek boys is well.

Dear Lissa, I wrote to you to send me some pants the first chance you get and the rest of them that I wrote for as I am nearly out of pants. There is a great excitement here today. They don't seem to think that we will stay here long. Some of them seems to think that we have to go to Winchester and some thinks that we will go to Staunton, but I don't know how it will be for there is so much news in camp. We expect a fight here of before long. Captain Long came to our cabin a few minutes ago and told us to be in readiness. You must excuse my bad writing as I am in a hurry and have no time to spend and bad ink and paper.

Dear and Dearest wife, you wanted to know if I was trying to get religion or not. I have been trying and I intend to try all that I can, but I tell you it is a hard place here in camp. I will tell you more about it the next time. You will please excuse me for this time, so nothing more but I will remain your affectionate husband until death. God bless you....

Tell all of the folks how I am and give my love to all my inquiring friends. I must bring my scribble to a close. May god bless you all. You will please excuse my bad writing for I have bad ink and bad paper and it is dark. I have some paper nothing more but remain your affectionate husband until death.

Fare you well.

H. H. DEDRICK to wife, *write soon.*

Captain Richard C. Derby, U.S.A.
Ball's Bluff, Camp Foster
Poolesville, Maryland
December 15, 1861

Letter to His Mother and Sister

It is a leisure Sunday, and I may as well write home as do nothing but read. We have had a sudden change in weather from south wind to north; but still the weather is not severe. My friend Clark writes that there has been some skating near Boston, but there has been nothing like it here. We have a good board floor in both our tents, and a cast-iron stove in place of our sheet-iron one, for convenience in cooking. It is a cross between our ornamental parlor stove and a useful kitchen ditto. We had a joint of beef cooked in the oven today. The prunes which you sent were very nice. I told Wesley (our servant) we could have some of them stewed for supper; and he cooked them all at once, and served them up in our largest oval platter in the center of the tea-table.

SUPPER TIME.

I will go up town some day, and see if the artist that keeps a "daguerreotype shop on wheels" can take a miniature on mailable material. If he can, I will send you one.... Ellen is just a little too late for a lock of my hair. I had it cut only a few days ago, and that's why I'm going to have my picture taken now.

I still keep possession of my fork. It was in my haversack with my spoon and case-knife. I put them in my pocket before I took to the water. I will enumerate the articles I had about me while swimming, just for your entertainment; and you will wonder I floated as long as I did.

The three items just named, my large jackknife, horn pocket-comb, about a half-pound of gold and silver coin, a package of envelopes, a large memorandum book, a handful of bullets, a metallic box of caps, a flask of powder, watch, and all my clothes except my boots. I ought to have saved my canteen as a life-preserver; but I did not think of it, and threw it away.

The report is that we are to have officers to fill the places of those who are prisoners. It will be a great relief, for we are very short for officers. The adjutant will take his place tomorrow, probably; but I shall not have to go on guard duty till I get through drilling the recruits.

Prof. Lowe [see note below] has been up here with his reconnoitering balloon, and made an ascension. I don't know that he made any important discoveries.

I have consigned my flying squirrels to the company kitchen. They were unsociable animals, and troublesome to take care of. They very seldom made their appearance till after candle-light, and then scud to their nests the moment any one attempted to make their acquaintance. In company K, they have an owl in a cage, and that is the latest pet.

Our chaplain is still in Massachusetts. He assists in recruiting, by delivering addresses in the towns of Worcester County.... You mustn't expect to see me home on a furlough this winter. Officers are not allowed leave of absence except on most urgent occasions. I thought, from the tone of Ellen's letter, she was hoping I should come home this winter. Give my regards to friends; and with love to all, I remain your affectionate son and brother,

Richard

Professor Thaddeus Lowe (1832–1913) was an inventor in charge of reconnaissance from a hot-air balloon for the Army of the Potomac.

Source: [YC]

1862

THE UNION ARMY IN SOUTH CAROLINA: *"your son proved himself a trooper in profanity at least"*

Captain Charles Francis Adams, Jr., U.S.A.
Beaufort, South Carolina
February 2, 1862

To His Mother, Abigail Brown Brooks Adams

...I was...in the delicious doubt of our first picket detail which I was to command. After all it didn't come to much and the only danger I had to face arose from the terror of my own horses at the sight of the sabres of my men and at the dulcet sounds of the band at guard mounting. Lord! what a time I had, and for an instant your son proved himself a trooper in profanity at least. But imagine the feelings of a young officer leading the first detail of his regiment ever seen at a public parade on seeing his men and horses go shooting over the field in all directions like squibs on the 4th of July. With stern decision I at once disgraced and sent home two horses and their riders and paraded the rest in style, marching them in review in a way which almost restored our honor. Then I escorted the officer of the day to his post and stationed my details and then visited the outposts.

We are all alone on an island here, and on its shores our pickets stand and gaze placidly at the pickets of the enemy on the shore opposite. About three times a week one party or the other try to cross in boats and get fired at, but no one ever seems to be hurt and so the danger is apparently not alarming.

I visited our furthest pickets and found them on Barnwell's Island at the house of Mr. Trescot, the author of whom we have heard. It isn't a pleasant picture, this result of war. Here was a new house on a beautiful island and surrounded with magnificent cotton fields, built evidently by a gentleman of refinement and very recently, and there was the garden before it filled with rubbish, and within broken furniture, scraps of books and letters, and all the little tokens of a refined family. Scattered over the floors and piled in the corners were the remains of a fine library of books of many languages, and panels and glasses were broken wherever so doing was thought an easier course than to unlock or open. I wandered round and looked out at the view and wondered why this people had brought all this upon themselves; and yet I couldn't but pity them. For I thought how I should feel to see such sights at Quincy....

Grandson and great-grandson of the American presidents John Quincy Adams and John Adams, Adams (1835–1915) graduated from Harvard in 1856 and joined the Union Army as a captain. His father, meanwhile, was serving as the country's minister to England.

Source: [CAL-1]

~

THE EVACUATION OF WINCHESTER: *"It was, indeed, a bitter thing to feel that our own army was gone, and then to see the Yankees in such numbers"*

Fanny Graham
Winchester, Virginia
April 3, 1862

To Mary Anna Jackson

My Dear Friend,—

...The events of the past few weeks have been so strange, so new, and so dreadful, that I almost feel as if I had entered upon a new existence; and when I sit and recall the pleasant hours that we passed together last winter, and the dear general's [i.e., Stonewall Jackson's] brief but happy visits to us, with all that delightful interchange of Christian and social intercourse, it seems like a bright dream. "Oh, could those days but come again!" I feel as though that would be almost too much happiness. The occupation of our town by the Federals came upon me like a dreadful shock. I had never permitted myself to believe for an instant that they would ever get here. I had a firm conviction that reinforcements were somewhere within reach, for, of course, we knew that our general, brave and splendid as he is, could not withstand an overwhelming force with his little band, but still I believed something would turn up to keep them away; and when he came to tell us good-by, looking so sad (and I know he *felt* deeply grieved), I felt stunned, and could scarcely trust myself to speak, lest I should say something to add to his troubles.

The agony of the next twenty-four hours, I trust, if it is God's will, may never be experienced by me again. It was, indeed, a bitter thing to feel that our own army was gone, and then to see the Yankees in such numbers, the main body marching to the music of their brass bands, but some tearing across the fields, up the alleys, and in every direction—"monarchs of all they surveyed"—it was too much for me, and I gave way completely. But I remembered that God reigns, and is *over all!* and I know this has not come upon us by accident. God has ordered and permitted it, and He has been better to us than all our fears. His angel has certainly encamped around our dwelling, and no harm has happened to us. It is really wonderful how we have been protected, while others have suffered so from their depredations. . . .

Our ladies have a daily prayer-meeting, which is very delightful, and serves to strengthen our faith and help us to bear our trials. I firmly believe that God will deliver us and drive out our enemies. Their sojourn among us has greatly increased the secession feeling, and persons who had never taken any part before have become violent. Indeed, the old town has stood up bravely for the South. This country is becoming completely desolated—the farms being stripped of everything, the fences all destroyed, and the farmers not planting any crops. There is no encouragement for them to do so, as long as the Yankees are here, for they take possession of everything they want. Their officers threaten to arrest every secessionist, but we are not intimidated, and I earnestly hope our general will come back before they have time. We do long and watch for the day when he will return at the head of his army, and we will give him such a welcome as no man ever did receive before.

Stonewall Jackson and his wife Mary Anna had stayed with the Grahams the winter of 1861–1862. This spring the Confederate troops had to evacuate Winchester.

Source: [MSJ]

~

Private Henry H. Dedrick, C.S.A.
Camp Shenandoah, Augusta County, Virginia
April 7, 1862

To His Wife, Mary E. A. Dedrick

My Dear Wife—

I received your kind letter yesterday. I was glad to hear from you and I was sorry to hear that you had the mumps, but if you take good care of yourself you will soon get well. I was glad to hear that Willie was so pert and so lively. I am well at present and I do hope when these lines comes to hand they may find you all well.

Uncle Will is not very well. He has been very sick. We have left Alleghany. We left last Wednesday and come to Monterey and the next day we come to McDowell and then we stayed there one day, and on Saturday we marched within a half of a mile of Rodgerses, which is on Shenandoah Mountain. We are now within 24 1/2 miles of Staunton and 14/12 miles from Buffalo Gap, but I can't tell you how long we will stay here, but if we stay here long I would like your pap to come out here to see me.

I would like to see you all very much, but if I can't get to see you before my time is out I think I can stay three months and a half yet if I have my health. All of the creek boys is well. William Diddle is sitting in his tent blowing his fife.

Dear Lissa, I was up on the top of a ridge yesterday and I could see the Blue Ridge. I could see the laurel and Spring Hollow and I said to myself now if I was up in that hollow how soon I could get home. Well, Dear Lissa, I will now finish my letter. It is now 3 o'clock and it is very cold and snowy. We all just have to do the best we can. We are nearly froze. All the balance of my mess is lying down in the tent wrapped up in there blankets. I wish you could see us, then you would say that we had hard times out here.

Lissa, you wanted to know how much I had to pay a year on that lot and how much I had to pay in all. I have to pay $38.75cts a year and there is four payments back yet that will make $155. Yet if you do pay any on it you must take in my note.

Uncle Will, Will Diddle, and Hiram Coyner and James Padgett and Ephriam Sillings all sends their best regards to you and Amanda and Aunt Rebecca and your mother and your Pap, and you will please give my love to all inquiring friends if there be any, and you must accept a great portion for yourself. You said in your letter that I had better kept one of them ladies that I sent you. I had no use for them as they could not cook nor wash nor do anything else. I would rather have you here by a long ways before I would have them. I must close as I am so cold I can't write. I was glad to get some of your hair. It is very pretty. May god bless you all. Nothing more but remain your affectionate husband until death.

See Mary Dedrick's reply of April 15, 1862, below.

Source: [VS] http://valley.lib.virginia.edu/papers/A6009 {Copyright 1999 by the Rector and Visitors of the University of Virginia}

~

SHENANDOAH VALLEY CAMPAIGN: *"You appear much concerned at my attacking on Sunday"*

Brigadier General Thomas J. (Stonewall) Jackson, C.S.A.
Shenandoah Valley, Virginia
April 11, 1862

To His Wife, Mary Anna Jackson

I am very much concerned at having no letter this week, but my trust is in the Almighty. How precious is the consolation flowing from the Christian's assurance that all things work together for good to them that love God!... God gave us a glorious victory in the Southwest [at Shiloh], but the loss of the great Albert Sidney Johnston is to be mourned. I do not remember having ever felt so sad at the death of a man whom I had never seen....

Although I was repulsed in the attempt to recover Winchester, yet the enemy's loss appears to have been three times that of ours. In addition to this, the great object which required me to follow up the enemy, as he fell back from Strasburg, seems to have been accomplished very thoroughly. I am well satisfied with the result. Congress has passed a vote of thanks, and General Johnston has issued a very gratifying order upon the subject, one which will have a fine effect upon my command. The great object to be acquired by the battle demanded time to make known its accomplishments. Time has shown that while the field is in possession of the enemy, the most essential fruits of the battle are ours. For this and all of our Heavenly Father's blessings, I wish I could be ten thousand times more thankful. Should any report be published, my views and object in fighting and its fruits will then become known.

You appear much concerned at my attacking on Sunday. I was greatly concerned, too; but I felt it my duty to do it, in consideration of the ruinous effects that might result from postponing the battle until the morning. So far as I can see,

my course was a wise one; the best that I could do under the circumstances, though very distasteful to my feelings; and I hope and pray to our Heavenly Father that I may never again be circumstanced as on that day. I believed that so far as our troops were concerned, necessity and mercy both called for the battle. I do hope the war will soon be over, and that I shall never again have to take the field. Arms is a profession that, if its principles are adhered to for success, requires an officer to do what he fears may be wrong, and yet, according to military experience, must be done, if success is to be attained. And this fact of its being necessary to success, and being accompanied with success, and that a departure from it is accompanied with disaster, suggests that it must be right. Had I fought the battle on Monday instead of Sunday, I fear our cause would have suffered; whereas, as things turned out, I consider our cause gained much from the engagement.

Source: [MSJ]

∿

COLD: *"no one knows how bad I want you to be in peace at home again"*

Mary E. A. Dedrick, C.S.A.
Rockingham County, Virginia
April 15, 1862

To Henry H. Dedrick, C.S.A.

Dear Husband—

I'll attempt to write to you once more to inform you of our health. I am well, only a pain in my back and side. Willie has been very sick with the Cholera Morbus. It weakened him down considerably, but he is now as mischievous as ever. I have had the same complaint that Willie had, but I have gotten over it.

It is a cloudy disagreeable day today. It has been raining here today but it has quit. I tell you, Dear Henry, my thoughts were fixed on you all them cold snowy days last week. I don't know how you poor fellows can stand it. I know you all have a hard time out

43

there in them cold cotton hats. I expect they will be many of you sick that haven't been.

Tears came twinkling from my eyes when I came to where you said that you came out on a hill and seen the Laurel Spring hollow and saying to yourself how soon could I get home if I was there. But I hope if it is God's will that you will be nearer home than that hollow before long. Dear Henry, no one knows how bad I want to see you. No one knows how bad it is to be from each other, only those that have tried it. But one thing I do sincerely hope that you may never volunteer again for no one knows how bad I want you to be in peace at home again.

I got a letter from Jack's wife and she wasn't very well. She expects to be confined soon. Jackson and Harry are in the army. William is at home on a sick furlough, he is getting better. I suppose Shenandoah has got a right nice little town on it chiefly of white houses. Tell me in your next letter how many regiments there are out there besides Baldwin's. I received the fifteen dollars you sent by Meyers. He came up to Lewis's. Amanda has the mumps but she is better (little Cate had them too). She sends her best and kindest respects to you and cousin William Diddle and to the rest of her friends out there and tell them their kindness were welcome received.

I was sorry to hear that you was so cold when you was writing and that you all was so cold. I hope if it is for the best that it will soon be pretty clear warm weather. Who did you send your coat and letters by. I haven't got them yet. I don't know whether Mary has got hers yet or not. I seen her yesterday but I forgot to ask her. Tell Uncle Will that she and the children were all well. Mother and pap are well. Pap tried to get us two calves over at old Gray's sale but they were too unreasonably high and he didn't get them.

Tears came in mother's eyes as I read her your letter. Pray a great deal, dear Henry, and never forget God...who has give you health, that you have been spared so long. "Pray without ceasing."

FROM YOUR WIFE M. E. D.

Source: [VS] http://valley.lib.virginia.edu/papers/A6020 {Copyright 1999 by the Rector and Visitors of the University of Virginia}

~

SIEGE OF YORKTOWN: *"This is the way some fellows act, in mischief all the time"*

Private Alfred Davenport, U.S.A.
Fifth Regiment, New York State Duryee Zouaves
Army of the Potomac
Camp Winfield Scott, Near Yorktown, Virginia
April 21, 1862

Dear Mother—

I received your kind letters of the 11th and 17th inst., and I can assure you was glad to hear from home, and that you were all in good health. We still remain in camp, and are as comfortable, that is for soldiers, as circumstances will admit. Our tents are of good material and keep out the rain, and the camp is situated on rather high ground, therefore the water runs off. To the south of our portion of the ground is a small ravine through which a small stream runs, supplied by pure springs, from which we get plenty of water for drinking and cooking purposes. In the stream itself we wash our clothes and ourselves. On the banks above the ravine there was a thick wood of pine, with their evergreen foliage; elm-trees, which were soon robbed of their bark to satisfy the chewing propensities of the men; sassafras bushes, the roots of which are pleasant to eat, and are therefore pulled up without regard to quantity; but the wood is now getting thinner every day, falling a sacrifice to our axes, and used by the cooks to keep up their fires, and by us as a means to warm ourselves when it is necessary. We can see the balloon make its ascensions every day, and once in a while we hear a report up in the air, look up and see a ball of smoke, resembling a small cloud, which tells us that a shell has burst in the air; but it is of such frequent occurrence that often we do not notice it. A few shells have landed in camp, one of which killed a mule; another was filled with rice, so they say; one fired yesterday cut a man in half—he was in the woods; but we are as safe as can be expected, and might stay here for forty years without being hurt; but about a mile further to the

45

By the Brookside

front I can't say the same thing, as there is sharp practice there on picket.

We see very little of Colonel Warren; he is with General McClellan and staff most of his time, making observations, etc., by whom he is highly esteemed. Many of the regulars know him, having seen him out West and other places, before the war. They say that he is a smart officer. We all like him, so far as a man and a soldier is concerned; he is strict, but he knows all the wants of a soldier from experience, and seldom taxes our endurance too much; but he may change—it would not be strange.

Our men are on details, night and day, building batteries and roads in every direction; one cannot tell at what time of night he may be called up to shoulder his musket, and march off on a detail. Saturday night I was on fatigue duty; we marched about three miles to the York river, where they are putting up a battery. Part of the road has been built by our army, leading over a creek through which a solid bridge has been built. As we came out of some woods at one point we could see a rebel fort (deserted, of course) in the middle of a swamp, to the right of the road; it was built square and in a substantial manner, with barracks inside, a ditch nine feet deep all around it, filled with water, and an abatis, bushes and stumps of trees. Near it was an inferior work, partially masked: the place could not have been stormed. Further on we went through the camp of the 1st Connecticut heavy artillery. We were astonished to see the heavy guns that have been sent to this point for the purposes of the siege. We next passed through the largest cornfield that I ever saw or heard of, and came to an extensive peach-orchard, which was in full bloom. Emerging from the latter, we came upon the grounds of one of the first families, on which was built a fine large house, with a waterfront on the York river. The battery we are building is a little way from the house.

The owner of this place is said to be a lieutenant in the rebel army now at Yorktown, and owns five thousand acres of land hereabouts. This place is certainly the handsomest one I have yet seen in Virginia. I, with others, was trotted off to the cornfield, to await our time to be called upon to take our turn at the pick and shovel, which was to be in about four hours. We accordingly stacked our arms, and sat down on the soft and yielding soil, to take it easy. In company with some others, I lit my pipe, and we sat there talking, trying to worry through the time, but it was not long before a storm, that had been threatening for some time, burst upon us with all its fury. It was rough enough for us, notwithstanding the joke went around as usual, and all tried to be merry, but it was under poor circumstances: we were all obliged to stand up side of our muskets, and take it all. The furrows between the hills of corn were filled with water, and we were all soaked through, muskets and all: the latter is always a source of anxiety to a soldier, as everyone knows that with a wet rusty musket he would stand a poor chance in case of attack. Finally our turn came to work; we fell in, and were soon hard to work in the mud and water, with very little light, so as not to attract the attention of Johnny Reb.

We worked about three hours, and were relieved, when I, with some others, succeeded in getting into a sort of kitchen of the mansion; we found a roaring fire in an old-fashioned fireplace, but every place that a human being could squeeze into was occupied. The boys were stowed away on shelves not over six inches wide, snoozing away as if they had no troubles in the world; some were sitting on barrels, asleep, in the cellar which led off from the room; others on the window-sill, and I saw one fellow trying to crawl under a refrigerator: in fact, it would have taken a New York detective to have ferreted them all out. In one corner of the room sat Hough, looking full of mischief; he is one of the leading spirits. Butch, the head devil, was not to be seen; he was stowed somewhere, and I warrant a comfortable place, if there was such a thing. Fuel becoming short, having burnt up several cot-beds, Hough says, "George, just put that mantel-piece on the fire: there are some more of them upstairs, I will bring them down." No sooner said than done; the mantel-piece was blazing away in no

Home Again

time. Just then a crowd of officers of all grades filled the doorway, with alarm on their countenances, saying that the chimney was on fire. The boys looked at each other, as much as to say, "We have done it now!" At the same time we did not care whether the house burned down or not, as far as the loss of it was concerned, but the truth was, it was a dangerous accident, as the rebels could have shelled us easily by the light; but the chimney was soon all right again, and everything went on as before.

A little while before this, the innocent Hough and the missing Butch had been scouting around on their own hook, to see if anything was to be made. They came across a pig-sty, the pigs in one end, and a lot of our boys in the other asleep. Hough grabs a grunter, Butch draws his knife across his throat in the dark. Hough lets go of him, and says he is a dead pig, when the pig makes off as fast as four legs can carry him. Butch finds out that in the hurry and darkness he used the back of his knife; they go after the others, but find them all flown. Trotting along, not in a very good humor at the loss of fresh meat, Butch spies a horse in a field: what does he do but drive him in a barn, where a lot of the boys are sleeping in stalls and on the floor; they all wake up, scared out of their seven senses, and it is some time before they will believe that the enemy have not been on them, and that they are all prisoners. This is the way some fellows act, in mischief all the time....

The battery we were working on is one of great importance; it is called Battery No. 1, and is built of gabions, and will mount two two-hundred-pounders, and four one-hundred-pound parrots, also two thirteen-inch mortars. It was commenced and put up within two or three days; the guns are brought up at night by a large truck, and will be mounted by tomorrow: although it has rained and stormed a cold northeaster for two days, the work has still gone on night and day; in fact, everybody is busy doing something.

A colonel of the rebels was taken the other day in a Maine regiment uniform; he was stopped by some of the very regiment whose clothes he was surreptitiously wearing. In reply to the question what regiment he belonged to, he replied the very one of his captors; they knew different, and marched him off to headquarters. A private of a secesh regiment also came into camp just after we arrived here, and asked for the 5ᵗʰ Virginia; he was forthwith nabbed: he had been away on furlough, and had not heard that Uncle Sam's troops had possession of the former rebel camp-ground.

Once in a while we have a chase through camp after a rabbit, but do not generally succeed in catching it.

The boys are greatly in need of tobacco, but I managed to get a handkerchief full of smoking—you know I don't chew—while out foraging on my own hook; it was a good thing I can assure you. Some of the captains supply the men from company funds, and Captain Partridge buys it himself, and trusts the men until they are paid. Our captain has company funds, but is so mean, he will not use it for any thing, he has never done any thing for the men, by which he would spend a cent of his own money.

I hope that the taking of Yorktown will be the means of stopping the war; and I think if General McClellan's plans succeed, that he will succeed in bagging the whole of the rebs. The Prince de Joineville was addressed the other day by the title of prince, when he immediately corrected the person who spoke to him, saying that he was a captain, and no prince here, in his broken language, and appeared quite angry.

I have had quite a cold for about two weeks past, and I cough some at night—I suppose that it will wear off as soon as warm weather sets in. There have been a number of men discharged already on account of disability—camp-life beginning to tell on them. Give my love to all, and write when you can.

YOUR AFFECTIONATE SON

P. S.—I forgot to mention the heroic conduct of a young man who for some time mated with me; his name was Walter S. Colby, and he came from Boston, I believe. He was sick when we left Baltimore for Fortress Monroe to take part in this campaign, and consequently left behind; he had a kind of slow consumption on him, and usually coughed all night. The surgeon, in Baltimore, after he got a little better, offered him his discharge, seeing that he could not live long, but he replied that he would rejoin the regiment and go home with it, or go home in a box. So, one day, who should join us on the march up the Peninsula but Colby; he was thin, but had come to stick it out, he said; and he did as long as he lived, which was up to Gaines' Hill. I never saw a man with a stronger will in my life, that was all that kept him up; he never dropped out on a march, while many a strong man failed to come to camp with the regiment. He was one day changing some of his clothes, and I happened to get a look at his lower limbs. I was horrified at the sight; I could have put one of my hands around either one of them; he was actually a walking skeleton, and how any man could do duty as he did, in such a state, surpassed all my reasoning. Well, at Gaines' Hill, poor Colby, while fighting bravely, was shot in the leg, which was very much shattered; as soon as he fell, he got up on the sound leg, supporting himself as well as he could on the shattered stump, took off his cap, and waving it in the air, gave three cheers for the Union at the top of his voice. He then became weak and flopped down again. One of the boys went to him, and asked him if he could do anything for him? He thanked him, and said that he would not live a great while anyhow, and he might as well die as he was, and that he had better not mind him, but look out for himself; so he took a drink of water, and we never after heard from him. I could enumerate many instances of presence of mind, and self-sacrifices amidst suffering; but you must wait till I come home, to hear of them, and then I will have much to tell—providing, of course, that God spares my life.

A. D.

Source: [SL]

∾

SIEGE OF YORKTOWN: *"Puritanical, selfish, thieving, God-forgotten, devil-worshipping, devil-belonging, African-loving, blue-bellied Yankees"*

J. Traviso Scott, C.S.A.
Company A, Sixth Georgia Volunteers
Yorktown, Virginia
Early May 1862

"To the Future Yankee Occupants of this Place"

We have retired to the country for a short time to recruit our health. We find that with your two hundred thousand men you are too modest to visit this place, and we give you an opportunity to satisfy your curiosity with regard to our defenses, assuring you that we will call upon you soon.

We hope a few days' residence in a house once occupied by men will induce enough courage in your gallant hearts to enable you to come within at least two miles of white men hereafter. Be sure to have on hand a supply of "pork'n beans" when we return; also, some codfish and "apple sass." When we learn to relish such diet we may become like you—Puritanical, selfish, thieving, God-forgotten, devil-worshipping, devil-belonging, African-loving, blue-bellied Yankees. Advise father Abraham to keep his Scotch cloak on hand, to keep soberer, and your wise Congress to hunt up two thousand five hundred millions of specie to pay the debt you have incurred in winning the contempt of every live man. We have on hand a few tools which we devote to the special duty of loosening the links of your steel shirts. Couldn't you get a few iron-clad men to do your fighting? Are you not horribly afraid that we will shoot you below the shirts? When are you coming to Richmond? Couldn't you go up the river with us? There is one score which we will yet settle with you to the death. Your fiend-like treatment of old men and helpless women reads you out of the pale of civilized warfare, and if rifles are true and knives keen, we will rid some of you of your beastly inclinations.

When you arise as high in the scale of created beings as a Brazilian monkey, we will allow you sometimes to associate with our negroes; but until then Southern soil will be too hot for the sons of the Pilgrims. The only dealing we will have with you is, henceforth, war to the knife. We despise you as heartily as we can whip you easily on any equal field.

Most heartily at your service, whenever you offer a fight.

Source: [API]

~

THOUGHTS OF HOME: *"How much pleasure there is in that word home?"*

Private Thomas D. Newton, C.S.A.
8th Louisiana Infantry
Madison County, Virginia
May 28, 1862

Sister Mary,

This evening, the 20th of May, affords me the delightful pleasure of writing to you all at home. Home. Home. How much pleasure there is in that word home? There is more than tongue can express. How oft have I thought of home. That place that I formerly so little appreciated. And to think of those that are there. The kind Father, the indulgent Mother to which I have been so disrespectful in days gone by. The fond sisters that I have so oft mistreated. Oh, that I could have my time over again how different I would live.

One may imagine something as to the ties that home has. Though, it is nothing compared to realizing the true state of things. I will tell you how much I think of home. That delightful home I have so often thought of the greater portion of my day in quietude enjoying the pleasures and comforts of life, and those that are dear to me. I think just enough of home to spend the remnant of my days, though they may be long, or short, in difference. There is of home a delightful place where one can have peace, and just rights with it. But, without those two items death is far preferable. I will stay in the field forever before I will have my country invaded. I will submit to the toils and hardships of camp. I will be found traversing the snow-clad cliffs of the Thoroughfare and the Blue Ridge Mountains first. I will endure the toil, forbear the pain produced thereby, before thinking of submitting to such tyrannical vandals as those negro-thieving, undermining, careless, unprincipled band of demons, which are really beneath the notice of the Devil himself.

I say and speak from my heart that life is sweet, though give me death before submitting to any such. Never has history, even in the days of uncivilization, not even the heathen when committing their brutal acts regardless of care, or Gospel, had to disgrace her pages with such detestable, disgraceful, disdainful, unprincipled stuff as the present in stating the whys and wherefores of this war, if it is truly accounted for. If it doesn't prove a disgrace to the Federals in the estimation of all nations, I can't see why. In short, to this end give me liberty, or give me death....

I can't think of anything else that will interest you. My health is fairly good at this time. You will write to me immediately to tell all you know of about Joseph and Isaac. I have not heard much from home in three months. Direct your letters to Oak Park, Madison County, Va. They will be forwarded from there to me. Write immediately.

Nothing more remains,

your warrior brother, until death,
Thomas D. Newton

Source: [CWH]

∿

THE BATTLE OF HANOVER COURTHOUSE: *"the sight was sickening and mournful, but we seem to look on these things as if we had been used to them all our lives"*

Private Alfred Davenport, U.S.A.
Fifth Regiment, New York State Duryee Zouaves
Army of the Potomac
Chickahominy River Camp
June 1, 1862

To His Mother

The last eight days have been trying ones to the regiment. We have been kept constantly moving, and were almost *starved*, sleeping on the road with no covering but an overcoat. We marched over eighty miles. Colonel Warren has command of our regiment, 1st Connecticut, 1,200 men, one of the finest body of men in the service, a Rhode Island battery of six pieces, and a regiment of cavalry were included. We went on an expedition the other day to destroy a bridge over the Pamunkey river, by which the rebels received supplies from the open country. We had a skirmish, and killed and wounded a few of the rebel pickets; the others *skedaddled*, and company H, headed by Col. Hiram Duryea, charged over the bridge after them; but they, being mounted, escaped.

An amusing incident occurred here: at the first shot fired by the rebels, as the ball whistled over our heads, a man in our company named ——, who was detailed in the surgeon's department, and on a march carried the box that contained our medical stores on his back, strapped on like a knapsack, at the first fire dropped on his knees behind a large tree, with his hands clasped in front of him, and his countenance showing every sign of terror. Now, this same fellow, in the seven days' retreat, made himself scarce, apothecary shop and all, and we never saw anything of him until about a month before our time expired. He had been hanging about hospitals and convalescent camps, and had joined *us* then to get an *honorable discharge*. This is only one of the many specimens of the curs that shirk duty and come to no punishment and receive government pay. There are thousands of them.

We came near being engaged in the Battle of Hanover Courthouse. A brigade of North Carolina troops stationed there under General Branch were surprised by Porter's corps, and after a skirmish retreated. We followed on in the direction of the firing; all of a sudden aides on horseback came flying by us, and we were ordered back again. It appeared that reinforcements had arrived on the cars to the rebels from Richmond, which runs right through the battle-field, and were advancing on our rear, and were actually then on the very place from which our forces had just driven Branch's brigade of rebels.

It was an immense wheat-field, about a mile and a half across. When we came back on it we wondered where all the troops had come from. All was excitement. They were moving on in "quick time" to engage the rebels who had just emerged from the woods which skirted the field of wheat.

Presently the "*music*" commenced just in front of us, in the wood. Our artillery did not get to work until they (the rebels) were on the retreat. General Porter did not send us in directly, and just before we did advance, General Butterfield rode up before, with his hat off, and told us to "do our best," and that he would see us supported.

We were all very tired from our previous expedition, but we advanced at a "double-quick," though some of the boys fell exhausted. We went into the woods and out across the railroad, but the rebels were retreating as fast as they could, and had got into another wood where we could not reach them, but the artillery in the road, sighted by General Griffen himself was firing at them and doing a great amount of damage. At every good shot the general patted the piece and said, "Well done! another shot in the same place." Soon the order came to cease firing, it being near night, and the battle was over, resulting in a complete victory for our side.

The 44th and 25th New York were fighting in the woods and suffered severely, but they said as soon as the rebs saw our red breeches coming through the woods they skedaddled. We had marched eighteen miles the day before, and at least thirty that day, and were completely exhausted.

When we came through the woods the sight was sickening and mournful, but we seem to look on these things as if we had been

The Bivouac of the Dead

used to them all our lives. I have often read descriptions of great battles, but did not realize or comprehend them until I saw the reality. The rebels were lying in every position along by a fence near a road, most of them dead: many of them when shot dead have a horrible look on their countenances, *as if they had seen something that had scared them to death.* I saw a father and son side by side, wounded; the old man was crying and trying to stop the blood that was flowing from his wound. They were both found dead where they were in the morning. Men get hardened seeing so much misery. In one place there were two or three found dead, that looked as if they had died talking together. All night we heard the moans of the wounded, who were undergoing surgical operations at a house near our bivouac.

The next day Colonel Warren, with *"ours,"* the 1st Connecticut, and the Lancers, made a reconnoissance on the same road as the rebels retreated on, to see if he could speak General McDowell's advance.

It was the object of the battle of Hanover Courthouse to open the way for General McDowell, but it seems he was kept back by the authorities at Washington. Had he been permitted to join us, there is little doubt but what Richmond would have been captured—at least it is the general opinion in the Army of the Potomac.

That night we marched back again to camp, sixteen miles—men strewn all along by the road, completely exhausted. Our checks were sunk in, and we had famine in our countenances. By some neglect of our regimental quartermaster, we ran short of rations, and consequently nature was supported on air.

Our camp is in a dense pine wood—a beautiful spot comparatively. We are liable to be called upon at any moment to go into the contest which is to decide the fate of one army or the other. We are so near the enemy that no drum or bugle-call is allowed to be sounded. The order was read off this afternoon to the effect that we were about to go into battle—that we were to leave knapsacks, wagons, and every thing on this side of the Chickahominy; to carry only haversacks, three days provisions, and canteens.

So you see the ball will open in a day or two. The men will all *fight well*—there is no mistake in that, and we will win; but the loss will be heavy. I will not have a chance to write to you for some time, and, perhaps, may never; but God's will be done. Now good-by, and love to everyone: hoping that God will give us the victory, and that we may crush out the rebellion, and that in my next I can say *"Richmond is ours,"*

I remain, &c.,

A. DAVENPORT

Source: [SL]

∼

RAIDING: *"Everybody says it is the greatest feat of the war"*

Lieutenant John S. Mosby, C.S.A.
First Virginia Cavalry
Richmond, Virginia
Monday, June 16, 1862

To His Wife

My dearest Pauline:

I have just received your letter this morning. I returned yesterday with General Stuart from the grandest scout of the war. I not only helped to execute it, but was the first one who conceived and demonstrated that it was practicable. I took four men, several days ago, and went down among the Yankees and found out how it could be done. The Yankees gave us a chase, but we escaped. I reported to General Stuart,—suggested his going down,—he approved,—asked me to give him a written statement of the facts, and went immediately to see General Lee, who also approved it. We were out nearly four days,—rode continuously four days and nights,—found among the Yankee camps and sutlers' stores every luxury of which you ever conceived. I had no way of bringing off anything. General Stuart gave me the horses and equipments I captured. What little I brought off is worth at least $350. Stuart does not want me to go with Floyd,—told me before this affair that I should have a commission,—on returning yesterday he told me that I would have no difficulty in doing so now. I met Wyndham Robertson on the street today. He congratulated me on the success of the exploit, and said I was the hero, and that he intended to write an account of it for the papers,—made me promise to dine with him today. I send you some captured things,—the carpet was in an officer's tent. . . .

There is no prospect of a battle here,—heavy reinforcements have been going to Jackson. . . . I got two splendid army pistols. Stuart's name is in every one's mouth now. I was in both cavalry charges,—they were magnificent. . . . I have been staying with General Stuart at his headquarters. . . .

The whole heavens were illuminated by the flames of the burning wagons, etc., of the Yankees. A good many ludicrous scenes I will narrate when I get home. Richmond in fine spirits,—everybody says it is the greatest feat of the war. I never enjoyed myself so much in my life. . . .

Mosby (1833–1916) became renowned as one of the most effective and fearsome of Confederate raiders.

Source: [JSM]

BATTLE OF SEVEN PINES: *"the enemy were so close up to the battery that every shot took effect"*

Sergeant John Whipple, U.S.A.
92nd Regiment, New York State Volunteers
White Oak Swamp, Virginia
June 22, 1862

To His Wife

Dear Lizzie—

We are still in camp on the Chickahominy, and in all probability will never be ordered to "the front" again. Casey's division is used up, and will, it is thought, never go into battle again; we got no praise for what we did at Seven Pines, although we held the field against desperate odds for a long time. McClellan gives us no credit for it. The battery which the Ninety-second supported fired 266 rounds of canister shot in less than an hour. A canister is a bag with 100 bullets in it, and 266 such canister shots give the number of bullets fired 26,600. As soon as the canister is fired it bursts, and the bullets spread in all directions; so you can imagine how many they might kill or wound. But this was only

CLEARING THE WAY.

60

one battery; there were others on the ground, and they were all busy I assure you; and another thing, the enemy were so close up to the battery that every shot took effect, piling up their dead in heaps. Besides this were regiments of infantry all firing as fast as they could. There were more dead on that part of the field than on any other. The secesh themselves admit that their greatest loss was there. Casey's division lost far more men than any other in proportion to their number; and yet, because we had to retreat before the superior numbers that threatened to outflank us and take us prisoners, and because that retreat was not conducted in a proper military manner, pacing over the ground in solid columns, with measured steps and military bearing,—while the enemy came surging onward like an ocean flood, threatening us flank and rear, and pouring in a storm of lead and iron hail upon us, before which our men fell like the forest leaves in autumn,—McClellan says we behaved shamefully. The men, in consequence, are discharged, and many swear that they will never fight again, for they do not like to be blamed after suffering what they have for their country.

The Ninety-second is about used up; most of the men are sick, and many of the officers have resigned. Our colonel was wounded in battle, and is not with us yet. Exertions are being made to get the regiment mustered out of service; whether they will succeed remains to be seen.

To give you some idea of our present situation, I will give you company I's report, as made out by your humble servant this very morning. At Potsdam we had one hundred: where are they now?

Absent, sick, 33; wounded in battle, 6; missing, 3; killed, 2; discharged, 18; detached service, 5; present sick, 19; present for duty, 5; died of disease, 9: total, 100.

Thus you see we have only twenty-four in our company here, and only five of those are able to do duty. The other nineteen are not very sick, but are worn out, and with needed rest and quiet they will soon be all right again. Other companies in the regiment are about as bad off. This morning, at inspection and dress-parade, the regiment mustered sixty-six men fit for duty out of nine hundred and fifty-seven that left Potsdam, N.Y. The fact is, we have not been used as we should have been, and the men don't care whether school keeps or not. So when they get on the sick-list they stay on it as long as they can, to get rid of duty. Our company had eight corporals and five sergeants, and not one of them is within a hundred miles of our regiment now except myself, the rest being sick, wounded, or dead. The three new corporals we put in are also used up; so I have all the business (which, in fact, is not very great) to do; and any day when we are ordered out on picket, or fatigue duty, or for drilling, myself as orderly sergeant, as in duty bound, report myself for duty; and, if need be, I get an excuse of the surgeon, and when I wish I report for duty again. I have to keep the company books, make out morning reports, detail the guards, take the sick to the doctor each morning, warn them out to drill, inspections, and parade, and see to things generally; and so, like all orderly sergeants, have to know far more about the company's affairs than the commissioned officers. As for standing guard, 1 have not done any of that important service for two months, having been acting company commissary when not engaged as orderly: that excuses me.

We have a nice camp; it would do you good to see it. It is in a pine grove, laid out in streets, and beautifully adorned with shade-trees. Our tents are raised on scaffolds of poles, two or three feet from the ground, to allow the air to circulate beneath. The streets are swept clean early each morning, and the dirt carried off in pails. We are not allowed to throw anything under the tents or in the streets; and take it altogether our camp is very pleasant and healthy. But the mailman is calling, and I must hurry. Dr. Kalt's boys are all well, except Stevens and Loure; but they are not very hard up. I have not heard from Court le Cooper yet. The Third brigade, General Palmer, has gone up. Palmer has gone into Church's division, and we, the Ninety-second, into the Second division. My love to all the friends. Yours as ever,

JOHN

Source: [SL]

～

62

GENERAL ORDER NO. 28: *"The devil had entered into the hearts of the women of this town to stir up strife in every way possible"*

General Benjamin F. Butler, U.S.A.
Headquarters, Department of the Gulf
New Orleans, Louisiana
July 2, 1862

To Mr. J. G. Carney, of Boston

My Dear Sir:

Many thanks for your kind note....

I am as jealous of the good opinion of my friends as I am careless of the slanders of my enemies, and your kind expression in regard to Order No. 28, leads me to say a word to you on the subject.

That it ever could have been so misconceived as it has been by some portion of the Northern Press is wonderful, and would lead one to exclaim with the Jew, "O Father Abraham, what these Christians are, whose own hard dealings teach them to suspect the very thoughts of others."

What was the state of things to which the women order applied? We were two thousand five hundred men in a city seven miles long by two to four wide, of a hundred and fifty thousand inhabitants, all hostile, bitter, defiant, explosive, standing literally in a magazine, a spark only needed for destruction. The devil had entered into the hearts of the women of this town to stir up strife in every way possible. Every opprobrious epithet, every insulting question was made by these bejewelled, becrinolined, and laced creatures calling themselves ladies, toward my soldiers and officers, from the windows of houses and in the street. How long do you suppose our flesh and blood could have stood this without retort? That would lead to disturbance and riot from which we must clear the streets by artillery, and then a howl that we had murdered these fine women. I had arrested the men who hurrahed for Beauregard,—could I arrest the women? No—what was to be done? No order could be made save one that would execute itself. With anxious, careful thought I hit upon this, "Women who insult my soldiers are to be regarded and treated as common women plying their vocation."

Pray how do you treat a common woman plying her vocation in the streets? You pass her by unheeded. She cannot insult you. As a gentleman you can and will take no notice of her. If she speaks, her words are not opprobrious. It is only when she becomes a continuous and positive nuisance that you call a watchman and give her in charge to him.

But some of the Northern Editors seem to think that whenever one meets such a woman one must stop her, talk with her, insult her, or hold dalliance with her. And so from their own conduct they construed my order. The Editor of the *Boston Courier* may so deal with common women, and out of the abundance of the heart his mouth may speak, but so do not I.

Why, these she-adders of New Orleans themselves were at once shamed into propriety of conduct by the order, and from that day no woman has either insulted or annoyed my line soldiers or officers, and of a certainty no soldier has insulted any woman. When I passed through Baltimore on the 23rd of February last, members of my staff were insulted by the gestures of the ladies there. Not so in New Orleans. One of the worst possible of all these women showed disrespect to the remains of gallant young De Kay, and you will see her punishment, a copy of the order for which I enclose is at once a vindication and a construction of my order.

I can only say that I would issue it again under like circumstances. Again thanking you for your kind interest, I am
Truly your friend

Butler's General Order No. 28 of May 15, 1862: "As the officers and soldiers of the United States have been subjected to repeated insults from the women (calling themselves ladies) of New Orleans, in return for the most scrupulous noninterference and courtesy on our part, it is ordered that hereafter when any female shall, by word, gesture, or movement, insult or show contempt for any officer or soldier of the United States, she shall be regarded and held liable to be treated as a woman of the town plying her avocation."

Source: [BFB]

∼

Major General George B. McClellan, U.S.A.
Commander, Army of the Potomac
July 20, 1862

To His Wife, Mary Ellen McClellan

...Which dispatch of mine to Stanton do you allude to? The telegraphic one in which I told him that if I saved the army I owed no thanks to anyone in Washington, and that he had done his best to sacrifice my army? It was pretty frank and quite true. Of course they will never forgive me for that. I knew it when I wrote it; but as I thought it possible that it might be the last I ever wrote, it seemed better to have it exactly true. The President was entirely too smart to give my correspondence to the public—it would have ruined him and Stanton forever. Of course he has not replied to my letter, and never will. His reply may be, however, to avail himself of the first opportunity to cut my head off. I see it reported in this evening's papers that Halleck is to be the new general-in-chief. Now let them take the next step and relieve me, and I shall once more be a free man....

Later.—... I believe it is now certain that Halleck is commander-in-chief. I have information this evening from Washington, from private sources, which seems to render it quite certain. You will have to cease directing your letters to me as Commanding United States Army, and let the address be, "Commanding the Army of the Potomac"—quite as proud a title as the other, at all events. I shall have to remove the three stars from my shoulders and put up with two. *Eh bien!* It is all for the best, I doubt not. I hope Halleck will have a more pleasant time in his new position than I did when I held it. This, of course, fixes the future for us. I cannot remain permanently in the army after this slight. I must, of course, stick to this army so long as I am necessary to it, or until the Government adopts a policy in regard to the war that I cannot conscientiously affirm—the moment either of these comes to pass I shall leave the service....

No position in the gift of the country can ever tempt me into public life again—my experience in it has been sad enough, but I have learned a useful lesson. I have tried to do my best, honestly and faithfully, for my country. That I have to a certain extent failed I do not believe to be my fault, though my self-conceit probably blinds me to many errors that others see. But one useful lesson I have learned—to despise earthly honors and popular favor as vanities. I am content. I have not disgraced my name, nor will my child be ashamed of her father. Thank God for that! I shall try to get something to do which will make you comfortable; and it will be most pleasant and in the best taste for me that we should lead hereafter a rather quiet and retired life. It will not do to parade the tattered remnants of my departed honors to the gaze of the world. Let us try to live for each other and our child, and to prepare for the great change that sooner or later must overtake us all. I have had enough of earthly honors and place. I believe I can give up all and retire to privacy once more, a better man than when we gave up our dear little home with wild ideas of serving the country. I feel that I have paid all that I owe her. I am sick and weary of all this business. I am tired of serving fools and knaves. God help my country! He alone can save it.

It *is* grating to have to serve under the orders of a man whom I know by experience to be my inferior. But so let it be. God's will be done! My conscience is clear and all will turn out for the best. All will turn out for the best. My trust *is* in God, and I cheerfully submit to His will....

McClellan was indeed tempted "into public life again" and again, eventually running for president on the Democratic ticket against Lincoln in 1864. He was the governor of New Jersey from 1878–1881.

Sources: [MOS] [GBM]

∼

BATTLE OF CEDAR RUN: *"If God be for us, who can be against us?"*

Major General Thomas J. (Stonewall) Jackson, C.S.A.
August 11, 1862

To His Wife, Mary Anna Jackson

On last Saturday our God again crowned our arms with victory, about six miles from Culpepper Court-House. I can hardly think of the fall of Brigadier-General C. S. Winder without tearful eyes. Let us all unite more earnestly in imploring God's aid in fighting our battles for us. The thought that there are so many of God's people praying for His blessing upon the army greatly strengthens and encourages me. The Lord has answered their prayers, and my trust is in Him, that He will continue to do so. If God be for us, who can be against us? That He will still be with us and give us victory until our independence shall be established, and that He will make our nation that people whose God is the Lord, is my earnest and oft-repeated prayer. While we attach so much importance to being free from temporal bondage, we must attach far more to being free from the bondage of sin.

Source: [MSJ]

~

NEW ORLEANS: *"I can go anywhere with you, I am not afraid of danger"*

Harriet Allen Butler
Lowell, Massachusetts
August 18, 1862

To Her Husband, General Benjamin F. Butler, U.S.A.

Dearest:

The news came this morning that the rebels have attacked Baton Rouge and been repulsed, that Gen. Williams had his head blown off by a cannon ball. Who is to take his place? Ah me, who have you left but Phelps, and he so unmanageable. New Orleans, if you

An Orderly Sketch from Life

can keep the fleet, is invincible; why do they go to Pensacola? I
sent you a letter this morning, would I could recall it, written from
depression I could not overcome. If it adds to your perplexities I
shall never forgive myself. Why did I not stay with you? It would
have been better for both of us. If we live to meet again we will
remain together. May there not be some mistake about Gen.
Williams? I believe he has a wife and children, what heartaches
all over the country! His death I must weep for, a truly noble
gentleman, always kind and courteous. What will you do without
him? An experienced officer is wanted at Baton Rouge if you still
hold it, and you have so few. Is it not wrong you should be left there
with so small a force? But yet you can hold it, New Orleans I mean,
against the whole south if they have not ironclad vessels to destroy
the fleet. And hold it you will, you are more able when pressed with
danger and with few resources. Use every precaution, and treat
Phelps kindly as possible. Oh, how much I wish I was with you!

Dearest, I can go anywhere with you, I am not afraid of danger,
but I cannot sit down apart and think; it unfits me for anything. I

hope you will not get this morning's letter until you receive this. I would not add a feather's weight by telling you I am troubled. The death of Gen. Williams has nerved me like steel. Would I were a man. I am stronger in the hour of danger, for then I forget myself and woman's cares, and feel all the high enthusiasm that leads to deeds of fame, and for this reason it is better I should be with you. I could never pull you back from what I thought it your duty to do, but should urge you forward, and help, with all the wit I have. I shall look for any news now. If you are firm as you will be, careful and far-seeing, the rebels cannot reach you.

Kiss me, dearest, and believe, me your

Affectionate Wife

Source: [BFB]

∿

The Second Battle of Manassas (Bull Run): *"it was a continual hiss, snap, whizz, slug"*

Private Alfred Davenport
Camp Near Chain Bridge, Virginia
Fifth Regiment, New York State Duryee Zouaves
September 3, 1862

To His Father

Dear Father—

I received, about an hour since, yours of 12th and 21st August, and some papers; also just before leaving Harrison's Landing, mother's and Carrie's of 10th instant, but have had, as you may surmise, no time or opportunity of answering them until now. We have not even had time to rest or prepare our food since leaving Harrison's Landing. Three days before leaving that place our knapsacks were sent away; since which time have had nothing but the clothes upon my back, overcoat, haversack, canteen, and accoutrements. I am now writing this with the stump of a pencil, the only one in our company, I believe; have no envelope, or anything to seal this with, but will trust to luck to close this some way. We marched from the Landing to Newport News in about three days and a half. The first day's march was one of the most severe that we ever experienced, being about thirty-five miles. We halted about a mile beyond the Chickahominy river, near its mouth, and were all exhausted, and about used up, and had to limp the last few miles, our feet being all blistered, and our limbs stiff.

At Newport News we rested a day or two, and were joined by a batch of recruits; took the steamer Cahawba, on which our brigade, consisting of our regiment and the Tenth New York, about 1,300 men, were crowded together for about sixty hours. I slept in a chair on deck, and hardly left it all that time, for fear I should lose even that berth. We landed at Acquia creek, and after some delay were crowded on platform and baggage cars; the one on which I was had no railing, and we sat with our legs dangling over the sides, and the centre of the platform crowded with our men, as best they could pack themselves. We reached Falmouth station after about an hour and a half's ride, and took up our march again; our arms being loaded, and sleeping under arms most of the time, often hearing heavy firing in the distance. We guarded several fords on the Rappahannock as we went along.

As we came near Catlett's station, we saw our wounded lying about a farm-house, and they were burying our dead of a fight the day before. Some rebels were lying by the side of the railroad track in their gore, dead. At that place two locomotives and trains were destroyed; also bridges, burned by the rebels. At Manassas the destruction of railroad property was complete, the remains of engines and their trains, stores, and clothing scattered in every direction.

From here we marched about eight miles, and drew up in line of battle, fired some dozen or so shell, but received no return; they were fighting some two miles below us, and there had been fighting in another direction the day before. We laid on the road that night, and the next day were at the scene of the previous day's fight, which it seems is what we call Bull Run; they were then carrying off the dead and wounded: we could distinguish the red pants of the dead of the Brooklyn Fourteenth, lying on a hill to the front of us, which was the disputed ground of the day before, our forces being driven twice from it, and soon to contain the dead and wounded of our own ill-fated regiment, of the same uniform as our Brooklyn brothers.

We took our position well to the front, on the borders of the Run, and batteries to the left and right, shelling from hills in the direction of the enemy; there was a hill that rose up directly in front of us. The rebels replied; his shot and shell came whizzing near us, sometimes compelling us to lie down. While this was going on, we gathered some dry brush, made our little fires, and boiled our coffee in our cups, which is our principal nourishment during our long marches. After lying here some time, we advanced in line of battle to the top of the hill, supporting a battery still keeping up the shelling: when I speak of we, I mean the Fifth and Tenth regiments, the regulars were further to the rear. We were in advance of the line of our army, and on the extreme left: finally we again advanced to a hill on our left, and a little in advance of our former position, our battery shelling away in an open space, in which the country could be seen for miles In that direction, our regiment drawn up facing the woods, our left resting on them, the wood running all along our front, and again at right angles to our rear on the left; the Run was at the foot of the hill, and directly in our rear, and only a foot or so deep at this place. Six companies of the Tenth were in the woods in front of our right wing, the remaining four companies being out as skirmishers. The rebels had hardly replied to our shelling for some time, and it struck me that mischief was brewing: two rifle-balls came near us, one of which was picked up by our orderly sergeant; it looked mysterious, as not a reb was to be seen. It was not long before a company of the skirmishers came in on our left, all much excited, huddled together in a heap: they were much scared, and looked as if they had seen a ghost; they said the rebels were coming on, and were right on top of us, on our left flank.

Before any orders could be given to change position, the balls began to fly like hail from the woods; it seemed as if the rebels had come out of the ground; it was a continual hiss, snap, whizz, slug. Pat Brady, who used to live opposite us in Lexington Avenue, in the wooden cottage, was the first one hit, he stood a few files

71

from me. He fell without saying a word, struck in the body; he was dragged a few paces to the rear, to be out of our way, by the lieutenant, when he undid his body-belt himself: he died there without a complaint.

On account of part of the Tenth being drawn up in front of our right wing, only the companies on our left could fire. We commenced, but the rebel fire was now murderous, our men falling on all sides, like grass before the scythe; the Tenth had already broke and were flying to the rear. We had not fired more than two or three rounds, before the rebels were on us in front and flank, their object being to surround us and take us prisoners; the order had been given to retreat, by Col. Warren, and save ourselves, every man for himself, but we did not hear it; the recruits began to give way, and then what was left of the regiment broke and ran for their lives;—the rebels after us, yelling like fiends; they were Mississippi and Texan riflemen, and were six to one of us; they came charging on, yelling for "Jeff Davis, and the Southern Confederacy!" They were mostly in their shirt sleeves, and looked savage enough. There was no hope, but in flight, of saving a man; all the time they were pouring in their deadly shots at short range; when we first broke they were not more than fifteen or twenty feet from us. The battery we were supporting got off safe, leaving Capt. Smead, its commander, dead on the field. He was one of our best artillery officers, and a graduate of West Point. Col. Warren and Capt. Winslow, acting in command of regiment, being mounted, got off safe, but it is a miracle that they escaped.

While running down the hill towards the Run, I saw my comrades dropping on all sides, canteens struck and flying to pieces, haversacks cut off, rifles knocked to pieces; it was a perfect hail of bullets. I was expecting to get mustered out every second; but on, on I went, the balls hissing by my head. I felt one strike me on the hip, just grazing me, and only cutting a hole through my pants. I crossed the Run in the wake of Col. Warren, he being about one hundred yards ahead of me, with his red cap in his hand, and his horse running at the top of his speed! I turned around to look behind once, and only once; that convinced me that it was no time to tarry. I saw two or three rebel officers on horseback, their swords drawn and

The Last Act of Friendship.

waiving their men on; it occurred to me to turn and fire on them, but I as quickly decided that it was folly, as I could not stop long enough to take any kind of aim, and I would become a mark for a score of rifles, so I kept on. The rebels came on and swept everything before them, completely turning the left wing of the army. There was no support whatever behind us, and somebody was evidently to blame; it looked to me as if it was left so on purpose to defeat Pope,—the old corps commanders of the army of the Potomac, being jealous of him, and not willing to co-operate with him.

When we rallied, there were about forty of our regiment, and were joined by lost ones of different regiments. We were glad to see our colors safe, and the remnant of our once proud regiment rallying around them. The wounded were coming hobbling along in droves, covered with blood; some being assisted by comrades, some carried in blankets, with a man at each corner, all talking at once, excited. The poor wounded, joggled about from one side to another; some of them yelling with pain: but such is war. Men and artillery flying, the horses galloping like mad, the drivers bewildered; officers with drawn swords and revolvers, shouting, cursing, threatening, no one to obey; bullets flying, shells bursting, the rattle of musketry and roar of artillery, every thing enveloped in smoke; aids and orderlies riding back and forth as if mad; here and there a general with anxious look, giving hurried orders to aids, and, all together, the din and confusion like pandemonium, such as we might picture to ourselves hell in the day of Judgment,—such is what we call a rout. All this commotion as sudden as a storm at sea after a calm. There we stood excitedly looking on all this scene, in an agony of suspense as to the fate of our army, and what the effect on our cause. There our little band stood, with but one will to obey orders, *but minutes were ages.* Lieut. Colonel Marshall of the Tenth, was exhorting and encouraging his handful of men with tears in his eyes, "Be brave and resolute men," said he, "come what will; and for God's sake, do not let me be ashamed of you!" But in a few moments we saw Gen. McDowell ride along the front, amid the storm of bullets, and soon a long line of men were seen through the smoke following in the same direction: the men went along at a double-quick and with a cheer; at the end of the line, I saw one of our red boys, going along with them, although he had no business there. I never heard who it was, and he probably left his body there. It was a whole division of troops sent to the rescue; our fate and perhaps that of the Union depended on their success, in staying the onward rush of the enemy.

Gen. McDowell's voice rang out clear and loud above the din—*"Let there be no faltering in this line!"* Immediately after a fearful rolling crash, as the whole division poured in their volley, succeeded by a fierce yell, told us that our boys had commenced the work of death, and were making a charge; at the same time some of our batteries on a hill opened with grape and canister on the rebel hordes. But darkness was fast spreading her mantle over the scene, and the army was saved. We immediately, under cover of night, commenced our retreat.

From the time the first shot was fired at our regiment to our getting off the field, it was not over fifteen minutes; yet in that time we lost eight out of eleven line-officers, killed and wounded,—they being all that we had left with us; among whom were Capt. Hagar, Capt. Lewis, acting major; Adjt. Sovereign, killed. We went in with about five hundred and eighty men, and now draw rations for two hundred and fifty men. Most of the recruits that had just joined us were either killed or wounded, having had no instruction, and not knowing by experience how to take common precautions. We have a lot more on the way to join us: little do they know what their trials and troubles are to be.

Our company, G, being on the left, next to the last company, lost heavily: out of fifty-eight men, we have twenty-four left, non-commissioned officers and privates. We only had one commissioned officer to command us, Second Lieut. Martin, as brave a man as I want to see; *he fairly cried when we broke*. I went off the field about the same time he did. How I escaped I don't know, but I thank God for it! There are now only eight or ten of two-year men left in our company, who were at Fort Schuyler when the regiment was first organized; the rest have been killed or wounded, sick in hospital, deserted, discharged, &c. We had then one hundred and one men in our company, and I can hardly expect to survive another such engagement, if we should be unfortunate enough to get into another. I fear it will wipe us out as a thing of the past, eight more long, weary months of marching and misery!

Oh! this is a dreadful war, and it is my conviction, one of extermination on the part of the rebels; they fight with determination, and all the prisoners we take seem to be confident of success in the end; they still persist that the South *will never give in;* some of the Texans drawled out in a conversation, "We will foute you until we are all dead, Yanks, and I reckon-then the women will foute you after that" (they say *foute* for *fight*). After the fight, we fell back to Centreville, which is strongly fortified, and by night we retreated to Fairfax, and from thence here, where we have just gone into camp, but how long to rest we don't know. The army of the Potomac is *most used* up, and requires rest.

We met Gen. McClellan on the road last night, who was on his way from Washington to meet the army. If any of his enemies and defamers amongst the "stay at homes" had been there, they would have held their heads in shame, at his reception; he has no enemies in the army, and the men would all die under him, if necessary. If he had been in command, there would have been no Bull Run No. 2! We were so glad to see him, that we cheered him until we were hoarse. He asked us how many men we had left, and seemed sorry at the reply; *we* were always favorites of his, and he always showed us off before visitors to the army.

All the stories of the numbers in the rebel army are no exaggerations, but stern realities, and a million of men in Virginia alone, at this time, are none too many to conquer the State; our people at home are too apt to underrate them, but they will find out yet by hard experience that they must exert all their power and bang together, or they will never conquer the South; I can foresee it. In relation to a position that you spoke about, I will simply state, that I can do my duty as a private as well, and with as much service to our cause, as I could if I was an officer; and when I look and think on the moaning wounded, and the stark dead, the thought comes to me, what are all worldly glories? Here lies an officer with his gaudy trimmings; a few moments before he was haughty and proud of the very traps that drew on him the deadly aim of the sharp-shooter! He is like the butterfly, who, with gaudy wings, attracts the eye of the school-boy to whom he falls a prey; he lies in the dust, with the more humble, though not less honorable private. Death makes no distinction, they are *both* now before their Maker!

I could not help noticing the country in our immediate vicinity, and that which we have recently passed through: the former, although mostly deserted, shows some signs of cultivation, not having been troubled by desolating armies for some months; the latter, all laid waste. It is devastation in every sense of the word, and must be seen to be realized. I hope to God that Government and the North will be able to put the rebellion down; but our Army of the Potomac, in its present state, dread the idea of being obliged to go over the same ground again with doubtful success. In fact, we sometimes fear that the South, like our Revolutionary sires, are determined not to be conquered; but if so, it is God's will, but we should never submit until all means are exhausted. Now I must close this somewhat lengthy letter; but I hope that you will have the patience to read it through, trusting that if the Johnny Rebs follow up their intentions of taking Washington, that they will go back with a flea in their ear. Remember me to all.

YOUR AFFECTIONATE SON

P. S.—I forgot to mention that we lost both of our color-bearers, and four color-corporals killed, and two wounded. One ran away. Sergeant Alison, who carried the United States flag, was shot through the arm; he gave the colors up to a corporal, and went about twenty steps to the rear, but came back again, appearing as if he was ashamed. Shortly after, he was shot through the heart. Sergeant Chambers ran up and rolled his body off of the colors, and bore them off the field. Sergeant Spellman, who formerly tented with me, and carried the State colors, was shot through his neck, so his food came out that way; his arm was taken off at the socket, and he was shot through the side in several places. Medical Director Howard tried hard to save his life, but he died trying to hum a hymn.

A. D.

See also Davenport's Camp and Field Life of the Fifth New York Volunteer Infantry: Duryee Zouaves. *New York: Dick and Fitzgerald, 1879.*

Source: [SL]

∿

ANTIETAM: *"It was a solemn time for me as I sat by the grave"*

Sergeant Silas P. Keeler, U.S.A.
8th Connecticut Infantry
October 6, 1862

Dear Brother—

I was surprised to hear of the death of Henry. I had heard that he was wounded, and got a furlough of two days to go and find him. Starting when your letter came to me, I wandered all day over the field at Antietam. I kept going for miles and miles, looking at every grave I saw, and was about to give up the search from fatigue and hunger (for I had already gone over twenty-five miles), but I kept on till dark, and just as I was about to lie down for the night, I saw a few graves under an apple-tree, a few rods off, and there I found the grave of our dear brother. It was a solemn time for me as I sat by the grave.

I found a person who watched with him, and was present at his burial. He was shot in the early part of the action. He died without a struggle. It will be a hard struggle for mother. To think he was taken away in so short a time after leaving home, while I have been engaged in six or seven battles! But the thought of his dying so peacefully (and no one can doubt his Christian character or fitness to meet his Maker), will lessen the grief of our mother, and brothers, and sisters. We have lost him; but this we know, he was a Christian, and showed a Christian spirit in all his actions. It seems like a dream. As I look from the "Heights" (Bolivar), I can see the rebel army, and a battle is expected in a few days. I am willing to meet them, no matter how hard the battle, or how long and forced the marches are, if we can only finish the war, or make a beginning of the end. I may too, like Henry, be shot down. If I die, I die in the faith of Christ, and have no fears as to what awaits me. I am happy wherever I am. I can lie down with as much ease, and rest for the night within range of the enemy's guns, knowing that at dawn we may meet face to face, as I could at home upon my bed. It is near midnight, and I must close.

Source: [SL]

❧

A RAID WITH J. E. B. STUART: *"The people in Pennsylvania were frightened almost to death"*

Lafayette J. Carneal, C.S.A.
Camp Near Martinsburg, Virginia
October 15, 1862

Dear Papa—

I write you a few lines to let you hear from me. I am quite well at this time and hope this may find you all the same. I have just returned from a scout with Gen. Stuart. We went through Pennsylvania and Maryland. We had a very good time and a hard

time. We were gone six days. The people in Pennsylvania were frightened almost to death. They thought we were going to kill all of them. Some nights we would travel all night. It was one of the greatest scouts Gen. Stuart ever took. We got plenty to eat in Pennsylvania. I enjoyed myself very well. In crossing back over the Potomac the Yankees were there to prevent our crossing but we drove them off and came across and did not lose a man. We got 40 prisoners and 140 (?) horses There was 3 shells fell within 15 feet of me but I did not get hurt at all. It seems that the Lord was on our side.

I must now close. My love to all. Write soon and send me shoes the first chance.

From
YOUR AFFECTIONATE SON

Source: [VS] http://valley.lib.virginia.edu/papers/F4050 {Copyright 2002 by the Rector and Visitors of the University of Virginia}

PRAYER: *"peace should not be the chief object of prayer in our country"*

Major General Thomas J. (Stonewall) Jackson
Winchester, Virginia
November 20, 1862

To His Wife, Mary Anna Jackson

Don't you wish you were here in Winchester? Our headquarters are about one hundred yards from Mr. Graham's, in a large white house back of his, and in full view of our last winter's quarters, where my *esposa* used to come up and talk with me. Wouldn't it be nice for you to be here again? But I don't know how long you could remain.... I hope to have the privilege of joining in prayer for peace at the time you name, and trust that all our Christian people will; but peace should not be the chief object of prayer in our country. It should aim more especially to implore God's forgiveness of our sins, and make our people a holy people. If we are but His, all things shall work together for the good of our country, and no good thing will He withhold from it.

Source: [MSJ]

~

WINTER CAMPAIGNING: *"Except in rains tents are wholly unnecessary—articles of luxury"*

Captain Charles Francis Adams, Jr., U.S.A.
First Massachusetts Volunteer Cavalry
Potomac Bridge, Near Falmouth, Virginia
November 30, 1862

To His Father, Charles Francis Adams, Sr.

Here we are once more with the army, but not on the move. We passed six days in Washington and it stormed the whole time, varying from a heavy Scotch mist to a drenching rain. Our camp was deep in mud, at times a brook was running through my tent, and altogether we were most unfortunate as regarded weather.

A Helping Hand

Still we succeeded in completing our equipment and I started
out on our new campaign tolerably prepared to be comfortable
in future. Nor did I, I am glad to say, waste my time while there,
but I fed on the fat of the land, feasting daily, without regard to
expense, at Buhler's. I no longer wonder at sailors' runs on shore.
Months of abstinence and coarse fare, cooked anyhow and eaten
anywhere off anything, certainly lead to an acute appreciation of
the luxuries of city life. It seems to me now as if I couldn't enjoy
them enough. While here I saw Aunt Mary repeatedly and she
seems much the same as ever. She was very kind and hospitable. I
also saw Governor Seward for an instant. He invited me to dinner
and was very cordial; but he looks pale, old and careworn, and it
distressed me to see him.

Here we remained till Friday evening, on which day the two
Majors and myself succeeded in getting paid off, after immense
exertion and many refusals, when we had our last dinner at

Buhler's and on Saturday, when we saw the sun for the first time for a week, we struck camp and moved over to Alexandria, on our way to join the brigade. We got into Alexandria by two o'clock and went into camp on a cold, windy hillside. We were under orders to join our brigade at Manassas, but when we got to Alexandria we found Manassas in the possession of the enemy and we did not care to report to them. Accordingly we sent back for orders and passed Sunday in camp, a cold, blustering, raw November day, overcast and disagreeable. The damp and wet, combined with the high living at Washington, had started my previous health, and now I not only wasn't well, but was decidedly sick and lived on opium and brandy. In fact I am hardly well yet and my disorder followed me all through our coming march.

Sunday afternoon we got our orders to press on and join the brigade at the earliest possible moment near Falmouth, so Monday morning we again struck camp and set forth for Falmouth. It was a very fine day indeed, but the weather is not what it was and the country through which we passed is sadly war-smitten. The sun was bright, but the long rains had reduced the roads almost to a mire and a sharp cold wind all day made overcoats pleasant and reminded us how near we were to winter. Our road lay along in sight of Mt. Vernon and was a picture of desolation—the inhabitants few, primitive and ignorant, houses deserted and going to ruin, fences down, plantations overgrown, and everything indicating a decaying country finally ruined by war.

On our second day's march we passed through Dumfries, once a flourishing town and port of entry, now the most God-forsaken village I ever saw. There were large houses with tumbled down stairways, public buildings completely in ruins, more than half the houses deserted and tumbling to pieces, not one in repair and even the inhabitants as dirty, lazy and rough; they stared at us with a sort of apathetic hate, seemed relapsing into barbarism. It maybe the season, or it may be the war; but for some reason this part of Virginia impresses me with a sense of hopeless decadence, a spiritless decay both of land and people, such as I never experienced before. The very dogs are curs and the women and children, with their long, blousy, uncombed hair, seem the proper inmates of the dilapidated log cabins which they hold in common with the long-nosed, lank Virginia swine.

To go back to our march however. Our wagons toiled wearily along and sunset found us only sixteen miles from Alexandria, and there we camped. During the latter part of the day I was all alone riding to and fro between the baggage train and the column. I felt by no means well and cross with opium. It was a cold, clear, November evening, with a cold, red, western sky and, chilled through, with a prospect of only a supperless bivouac, a stronger home feeling came over me than I have often felt before, and I did sadly dwell in my imagination on the intense comfort there is in a thoroughly warm, well-lighted room and well-spread table after a long cold ride. However I got into camp before it was dark and here things were not so bad. The wind was all down, the fires were blazing and we had the elements of comfort. The soup Lou sent me supplied me with a hot supper—in fact I don't know what I should have done if it had not been for that, through this dreary march; and after that I spread my blankets on a bed of fir-branches close to the fire and slept as serenely as man could desire to sleep.

The next morning the weather changed and it gradually grew warmer and more cloudy all day. Our road lay through Dumfries and became worse and worse as we pushed along, until after making only eight miles, we despaired of our train getting along and turned into an orchard in front of a deserted plantation house and there camped. Our wagons in fact did get stuck and passed the night two miles back on the road, while we built our fires and made haste to stretch our blankets against the rain. It rained hard all night, but we had firewood and straw in plenty, and again I slept as well as I wish to.

Next day the wagons did not get up until noon and it was two o'clock before we started. Then we pushed forward until nearly dark. An hour before sunset we came up with the flank of the army resting on Acquia Creek. We floundered along through the deep red-mud roads till nearly dark and then, having made some five miles, turned into a beautiful camping ground, where we once more bivouacked. One thing surprises me very much and that is the very slight hardship and exposure of the bivouac. Except in rains tents are wholly unnecessary—articles of luxury.

Here, the night before Thanksgiving and cold at that, I slept as soundly and warmly before our fire as I could have done in bed at home. The reason is plain. In a tent one, more or less, tries to undress; in the bivouac one rolls himself, boots, overcoat and all, with the cape thrown over his head, in his blankets with his feet to the fire, which keeps them warm and dry, and then the rest will not trouble him. A tent is usually equally cold and also very damp.

The next day was Thanksgiving Day—27th November. It was a fine clear day, with a sharp chill in the little wind which was stirring. I left the column and rode forward to General Hooker's Head Quarters through the worst roads I ever saw, in which our empty wagons could hardly make two miles an hour. I saw General Hooker and learnt the situation of our brigade, and here too we came up with our other battalion. We passed them however and came over here to our present camp, where we have pitched our tents and made ourselves as comfortable as we can while we await the course of events.

As to the future, you can judge better than I. I have no idea that a winter campaign is possible in Virginia. The mud is measured already by feet, and the rains have hardly begun. The country is thoroughly exhausted and while horses can scarcely get along

Running the Gauntlet

alone, they can hardly succeed in drawing the immense supply and ammunition trains necessary for so large an army, to say nothing of the artillery which will be stuck fast. The country may demand activity on our part, but mud is more obdurate than popular opinion, and active operations here I cannot but consider as closed for the season. As to the army, I see little of my part of it but my own regiment. I think myself it is tired of motion and wants to go to sleep until the spring. The autumn is depressing and winter hardships are severe enough in the most comfortable of camps. Winter campaigns may be possible in Europe, a thickly peopled country of fine roads, but in this region of mud, desolation and immense distances, it is another matter.

Source: [CAL-1]

~

A BABY DAUGHTER: *"Give her many kisses for her father"*

Major General Thomas J. (Stonewall) Jackson, C.S.A.
Near Guiney's Station, Virginia
December 4, 1862

To His Wife, Mary Anna Jackson

Oh! how thankful I am to our kind Heavenly Father for having spared my precious wife and given us a little daughter! I cannot tell you how gratified I am, nor how much I wish I could be with you and see my two darlings. But while this pleasure is denied me, I am thankful it is accorded to you to have the little pet, and I hope it may be a great deal of company and comfort to its mother. Now don't exert yourself to write to me, for to know that you were taxing yourself to write would give me more pain than the letter would pleasure, so *you must not do it*. But you must *love your esposo* in the meantime.... I expect you are just made up now with that baby. Don't you wish your husband wouldn't claim any part of it, but let you have the sole ownership? Don't you regard it as the most precious little creature in the world? Do not spoil it, and don't let anybody tease it. Don't permit it to have a bad temper.

85

How I would love to see the darling little thing! Give her many kisses for her father.

At present I am about fifty miles from Richmond, and one mile from Guiney's Station, on the railroad from Richmond to Fredericksburg. Should I remain here, I do hope you and baby can come to see me before spring, as you can come on the railroad. Wherever I go, God gives me kind friends. The people here show me great kindness. I receive invitation after invitation to dine out, and spend the night, and a great many provisions are sent me, including nice cakes, tea, loaf-sugar, etc., and the socks and gloves and handkerchiefs still come!

I am so thankful to our ever-kind Heavenly Father for having so improved my eyes as to enable me to write at night. He continually showers blessings upon me; and that you should have been spared, and our darling little daughter given us, fills my heart with overflowing gratitude. If I know my unworthy self, my desire is to live *entirely and unreservedly to God's glory.* Pray, my darling, that I may so live.

Source: [MSJ]

~

THE BIVOUAC FIRE: *"My enjoyment springs from the open air sense of freedom and strength"*

Captain Charles Francis Adams, Jr., U.S.A.
First Massachusetts Volunteer Cavalry
Potomac Run, Near Falmouth, Virginia
December 9, 1862

To His Mother, Abigail Brown Brooks Adams

After a day or night of duty, it is strange what a sense of home and home comfort one attaches to the bivouac fire. You come in cold, hungry and tired and I assure you all the luxuries of home scarcely seem desirable beside its bright blaze, as you polish off a hot supper. And such suppers! You've no idea how well we live, now we've added experience to hunger. This evening, I remember, I had army-bread fried in pork—and some day I'll let you know what can be made of that dish—hot coffee, delicate young roast pig, beefsteak and an arrangement of cabbage, from the tenement of a neighboring mud-sill. This, with a pipe of tobacco, a bunk of fir branches well lined with blankets and a crackling fire before it left little to be desired. There is a wild luxury about it, very fascinating to me, though I never realize the presence of danger and that excitement which some men derive from that; to me camp always seems perfectly secure and my horses kick and champ on the other side of my fire, and my arms hang on the ridge of my bunk, practically as little thought of by me as though the one were in the stable at Quincy, and the other hanging over my mantelpiece in Boston. My enjoyment springs from the open air sense of freedom and strength. It's a lawless sort of feeling, making me feel as if I depended only on nature and myself for enjoyment.

This is all very well when the weather is fine, even in December; but next morning a change came o'er me, for early in the morning it began to rain and snow and, by the time we were relieved, at noon it snowed most heartily, so that I sincerely

A Roadside Argument.

pitied the miserable creatures who relieved us. Home we rode, wet and cold, and as I walked sulkily along, I tried to think of one crumb of comfort awaiting me when I got back into camp. I couldn't think of one, unless indeed the commissary might have procured some whiskey. Wrong again! I got into camp and found Colonel Sargent there with three companies from Hooker's headquarters and things looked lively enough, though far from cheerful, and as luck would have it Henry Davis was there, established in the midst of discomfort in his usual comfort. So I passed the evening with him, cursing Colonel —— (in which chorus we all unanimously concur), smoking the best of tobacco, drinking hot whiskey punch and eating plum-cake fresh from Washington....

Source: [CAL-1]

~

GRIEF: *"sorrow comes to all; and, to the young, it comes with bitterest agony"*

President Abraham Lincoln
Washington, D.C.
December 23, 1862

To Miss Fanny McCullough

Dear Fanny,

It is with deep grief that I learn of the death of your kind and brave Father; and, especially, that it is affecting your young heart beyond what is common in such cases. In this sad world of ours, sorrow comes to all; and, to the young, it comes with bitterest agony, because it takes them unawares. The older have learned to ever expect it. I am anxious to afford some alleviation of your present distress. Perfect relief is not possible, except with time. You can not now realize that you will ever feel better. Is not this so? And yet it is a mistake. You are sure to be happy again. To know this, which is certainly true, will make you some less miserable now. I have had experience enough to know what I say; and you need only to believe it, to feel better at once. The memory of your dear Father, instead of an agony, will yet be a sad sweet feeling in your heart, of a purer, and holier sort than you have known before.

Please present my kind regards to your afflicted mother.

Your sincere friend
A. LINCOLN

Fanny's father, Lieutenant Colonel William McCullough of the 4th Illinois Cavalry, was a friend of Lincoln's and died in battle in Mississippi on December 5, 1862.

Source: [AL]

∽

CHRISTMAS: *"But what a cruel thing is war!"*

General Robert E. Lee, C.S.A.
Commander, Army of Northern Virginia
Camp Fredericksburg, Virginia
December 25, 1862

To His Wife, Mary Lee

I will commence this holy day, dearest May, by writing to you. My heart is filled with gratitude to Almighty God for his unspeakable mercies, for which he has blessed us on this day, for those he has granted us from the beginning of life, and particularly for those he has vouchsafed us during the past year. What should have become of us without his crowning help and protection? I have seen his hand in all the events of the war. Oh, if our people would only recognize it and cease from their vain self-boasting and adulations, how strong would be my belief in final success and happiness to our country! For in Him alone I know is our trust and safety. Cut off from all communication with you and my children, my greatest pleasure is to write to you and them. Yet I have no time to indulge in it. You must tell them so, and say that I continually think of them and love them fervently with all my heart. They must write to me without waiting for replies. I shall endeavor to write to Mildred, from whom I have not heard for a long time. Tell dear Charlotte I have rec'd her letter and feel greatly for her. I saw her Fitzhugh this morning, with his young aide, riding at the head of his brigade, on his way up the Rappahannock. I regret so he could not get to see her. He only got her letter I enclosed him last week. She ought not to have married a young soldier....

F. and R. were very well. But what a cruel thing is war! To separate and destroy families and friends and mar the present joys and happiness God has granted us in this world. To fill our hearts with hatred instead of love for our neighbors, and to devastate the fair face of this beautiful world. I pray that on this day, when "peace and good will" are preached to all mankind, that better thoughts will fill the hearts of our enemies and turn them to peace. The confusion that now exists in their counsels will thus result in good. Our army was never in such good health and condition since I have been attached to it, and I believe they share with me my disappointment that the enemy did not renew the combat on the 13th. I was holding back all that day and husbanding our strength and ammunition for the great struggles for which I thought he was preparing. Had I divined that was to be his only effort, he would have had more of it. But I am content. We might have gained more, but we would have lost more, and perhaps our relative condition would not have been improved. My heart bleeds at the death of every one of our gallant men. Give much love to every one.

Kiss Chass and Agnes for me, and believe me with true affection yours.

~

FINDING HIS BROTHER: *"One of the first things that met my eyes in camp, was a heap of feet, arms, legs, and under a tree in front a hospital"*

Walt Whitman
Washington, D. C.
Monday forenoon, December 29, 1862

To His Mother, Louisa Van Velsor Whitman

Dear, dear Mother,

Friday the 19th inst. I succeeded in reaching the camp of the 51st New York, and found George alive and well—In order to make sure that you would get the good news, I sent back by messenger to Washington (I dare say you did not get it for some time) a telegraphic dispatch, as well as a letter—and the same to Hannah at Burlington. I have staid in camp with George ever since, till yesterday, when I came back to Washington—about the 24th George got Jeff's letter of the 20th. Mother, how much you must have suffered, all that week, till George's letter came—and all the rest must too. As to me, I know I put in about three days of the greatest suffering I ever experienced in my life. I wrote to Jeff how I had my pocket picked in a jam and hurry, changing cars, at Philadelphia, so that I landed here without a dime. The next two days I spent hunting through the hospitals, walking all day and night, unable to ride, trying to get information, trying to get access to big people, and—I could not get the least clue to anything—Odell would not see me at all—But Thursday afternoon, I lit on a way to get down on the government boat that runs to Aquia creek, and so by railroad to the neighborhood of Falmouth, opposite Fredericksburgh—So by degrees I worked my way to Ferrero's brigade, which I found Friday afternoon without much trouble after I got in camp. When I found dear brother George, and found that he was alive and well, O you may imagine how trifling all my little cares and difficulties seemed—they vanished into nothing. And now that I have lived for eight or nine days amid such scenes as the camps furnish, and had a practical part in it all, and realize the way that hundreds of thousands of good men are now living, and have had to live for a year or more, not only without any of the comforts, but with death and sickness and hard marching and hard fighting, (and no success at that,) for their continual experience—really nothing we call trouble seems worth talking about. One of the first things that met my eyes in camp, was a heap of feet, arms, legs, and under a tree in front a hospital, the Lacy house.

George is very well in health, has a good appetite—I think he is at times more wearied out and homesick than he shows, but stands it upon the whole very well. Every one of the soldiers, to a man, wants to get home.

I suppose Jeff got quite a long letter I wrote from camp, about a week ago. I told you that George had been promoted to Captain—his commission arrived while I was there. . . .

Jeff must write oftener, and put in a few lines from mother, even if it is only two lines—then in the next letter a few lines from Mat, and so on. You have no idea how letters from home cheer one up in camp, and dissipate homesickness.

News from the Yanks

While I was there George still lived in Capt. Francis's tent—there were five of us altogether, to eat, sleep, write, and in a space twelve feet square, but we got along very well—the weather all along was very fine—and would have got along to perfection, but Capt. Francis is not a man I could like much—I had very little to say to him. George is about building a place, half-hut and half-tent, for himself—(he is probably about it this very day)—and then he will be better off, I think. Every Captain has a tent, in which he lives, transacts company business, and has a cook, (or man of all work,) and in the same tent mess and sleep his Lieutenants, and perhaps the 1st sergeant. They have a kind of fire-place, and the cook's fire is outside, on the open ground. George had very good times while Francis was away—the cook, a young disabled soldier, Tom, is an excellent fellow, and a first-rate cook, and the 2nd Lieutenant, Pooley, is a tip-top young Pennsylvanian. Tom thinks all the world of George—when he heard he was wounded, on the day of the battle, he left every thing, got across the river, and went hunting for George through the field, through thick and thin. I wrote to Jeff that George was wounded by a shell, a gash in the cheek—you could stick a splint through into the mouth, but it has healed up without difficulty already. Every thing is uncertain about the army, whether it moves or stays where it is. There are no furloughs granted at present. I will stay here for the present, at any rate long enough to see if I can get any employment at any thing, and shall write what luck I have. Of course I am unsettled at present.

Dear mother, my love,
WALT

The greatest poet of "the American experience" was forty-one and living in Brooklyn when the war broke out. After his younger brother George (born 1829) joined the 51st New York Volunteers and was reported wounded after the Battle of Fredericksburg, Whitman left New York to search for him, and thus began his two years of attention and service to the wounded and dying soldiers in the hospitals of Washington, D.C.

Source: [WD]

The hungry edge of appetite

1863

Wounded: *"I ran around till my boot was full of blood"*

Private Dwight A. Lincoln
42nd Illinois Volunteers
Nashville, Tennessee
January 10, 1863

Dear Father—

I received your kind letter at Nashville, after having marched all day through cornfields and mud, expecting to have a fight every moment; but lo and behold, the enemy were gone, and we went into camp, wet through and nothing scarcely to eat. But the next day we had an abundance. The next day we started for Murfreesboro, and arrived at night as near there as we thought it healthy to go. But we were not allowed to have any fire, so we had to make a supper of a few pieces of crackers. The next morning we got up all wet, it having rained in the night. We ate what we had left in our haversacks, and started our brigade in advance.

We did not go more than a mile before we were stopped by the enemy. Our regiment was thrown out as skirmishers. We *"skirmished"* most of the day. Night came, and not having had any dinner, we had nothing for supper. A hog made his appearance, and we soon dispatched him. We had no time to cook it before we were called to go on picket. We went; lay on the ground four hours; and liked to have shook ourselves to death with cold; came back to the reserves, cooked some meat and ate it, and then lay down till morning.

In the morning we were relieved, and took our position in line of battle, when some meat and mush were brought up. We had hardly time to eat it before we were called on to make a charge on the enemy. We started, and had only gone a short distance before a man, who stood beside me in the ranks, was shot dead. On we went, the boys cheering, and the enemy peppering us and falling back. We drove them, and regained our old ground, which was covered by dead and wounded. Just at this time the men on our right gave way; so of course we had to retreat. In the charge, which was made across an open field, we had five wounded and one killed. The fighting after this was terrific. Our division was at one time surrounded on three sides. It was about this time that I was wounded. Colonel Roberts was shot dead a few paces behind me. I ran around till my boot was full of blood, and saw it was no use, so I lay down and was taken prisoner. I was held four days, during which time I had two small biscuits a day to eat, and it was over a day before my wound was looked to or washed. I am wounded in the left knee, the bone being a little shattered. It is a pretty bad wound, but I guess it will heal if nothing befalls it. If the ball had struck an inch and a half higher, it would have been all day with me. The brigade doctor said it was as narrow an escape as I would ever have.

The rebels forgot to parole the wounded in the tent I was in, so I am not paroled. Much love to all.

From your son,
DWIGHT A. LINCOLN

Private Lincoln died ten days later in a Nashville hospital.

Source: [SL]

∾

BATTLE OF STONE RIVER: *"more lives were lost in two hours there, than in the same time during the war"*

W. H. Timberlake, U.S.A.
81st Regiment, Indiana Volunteers
Murfreesboro, Tennessee
January 12, 1863

To [Unknown]—

We had a desperate battle here. For four days the fortunes of war seemed to be against us, but Providence at last turned the scales in our favor. I can yet seem to hear the din of the conflict—the whiz of the bullet, the scream, of the shell, and the roar of the artillery! It is yet with me like one who has been on the sea; he becomes so accustomed to the roll and pitch of the ship, that it seems when on shore that the very earth is upheaving beneath his tread.

Our regiment was in the commencement of the bloody battle of Wednesday (December 31st), when our right was turned. General Jefferson C. Davis commands the division, and we stood the full shock of their concentrated charge.

Defending a Battery

General Johnson, who commanded a division adjoining us, suffered himself to be surprised and routed, thereby very nearly losing us the battle and causing the army to be annihilated. It seemed as if all were lost on that Wednesday. The enemy having massed their forces, or nearly all their whole force, against our right wing, commanded by McCook, swept over it like an avalanche! There was no resisting it. Our brigade gained more honor than any other on the right; but *we* had to fall back, leaving killed and wounded in their hands. Everything went against us that day, and nearly everyone prayed for night to come, that we might *retreat*. But Rosecrans knows no such word.

Thursday.—No advantage on either side, but the carnage terrible! Friday.—The battle commenced at two o'clock, and I venture to say more lives were lost in two hours there, than in the same time during the war. The enemy attacked our left wing, which resisted stubbornly, but, like ourselves, had to fall back from loss of numbers, but not until they had made sad havoc among the enemy.

As they fell back, General Negley threw his division forward, while our artillery was concentrated against their ranks. Then the rebels lost; they were literally mowed down! They had such an immense force, however, that Negley could not drive them. His men and the rebels were very much disorganized in the hand to hand conflict, when orders were brought to our general to "forward with his division, and make a charge!"

Away we went, "double-quick," or rather, "on the run"; forded a stream over knee-deep three times; charged up the hill, where the rebels were, with a yell, and the rebs, panic-stricken, threw away their arms and fled. Such a sight as we saw! The ground was covered with the dead and dying.

The rebels admitted their loss in that one charge to be 800! This was the decisive blow of the battle. That night they commenced their retreat. But, in the four days' fight, with two days of heavy rain, cold, without blankets, no fires, and scarcely any sleep, our forces were entirely too exhausted to pursue.

How near we came to being defeated, only those who saw can realize.

Source: [SL]

~

DOUBT: *"I now lament extremely my early education and life"*

Captain Charles Francis Adams, Jr., U.S.A.
First Massachusetts Volunteer Cavalry
Potomac River, Virginia
January 23, 1863

To His Brother, Henry Adams

I do wish you took a little more healthy view of life. You say "whether my present course of life is profitable or not I am very sure yours is not." Now, my dear fellow, speak for yourself. Your life may be unprofitable to you, and if it is, I shall have my own ideas as to why it is so; but I shall not believe it is until I see it from my own observation. As to me my present conviction is that my life is a good one for me to live, and I think your judgment will jump with mine when next we meet. I can't tell how you feel about yourself, but I can how I feel about myself, and I assure you I have the instinct of growth since I entered the army. I feel within myself that I am more of a man and a better man than I ever was before, and I see in the behavior of those around me and in the faces of my friends, that I am a better fellow. I am nearer other men than I ever was before, and the contact makes me more human. I am on better terms with my brother men and they with me. You may say that my mind is lying fallow all this time. Perhaps, but after all the body has other functions than to carry round the head, and a few years' quiet will hardly injure a mind warped, as I sometimes suspect mine was, in time past by the too constant and close inspection of print.

I never should have suspected it in time past, but to my surprise I find this rough, hard life, a life to me good in itself. After being a regular, quiet respectable stay-at-home body in my youth, lo! at twenty-seven I have discovered that I never knew myself and that nature meant me for a Bohemian—a vagabond. I am growing and developing here daily, but in such strange directions. Let not my father try to tempt me back into my office and the routine of business, which now seems to sit like a terrible incubus on my past. No! he must make up his mind to that. I hope my late letters have paved the way to this conviction with him. If not, you may as well break it to him gently; but the truth is that going back to Boston and its old treadmill is one of the aspects of the future from which my mind fairly revolts. With the war the occupation of this Othello's gone, and I must hit on a new one. I don't trouble myself much about the future, for I fear the war will not be over for years to come. Of course I don't mean this war, in its present form: that we all see is fast drawing to a close; but indications all around point out to me a troubled future in which the army will play an important part for good or evil, and needs to be influenced accordingly. I shall cast my fate in with the army and the moment reorganization takes place on the return of peace and the disbandment of volunteers I shall do all I can to procure the highest grade in the new army for which I can entertain any hope.

I now lament extremely my early education and life. I would I had been sent to boarding school and made to go into the world and mix with men more than my nature then inclined me to. I would I had been a venturous, restive, pugnacious little black-guard, causing my *pa-r-i-ents* much mental anxiety. In that case I should now be an officer not at all such as I am. But after all it isn't too late to mend and enough active service may supply my deficiencies of education still. Meanwhile here I am, and here I am contented to remain. The furlough fever has broken out in our regiment, and the officers, right and left, are figuring up how they can get home for a time. Three only of us are untouched and declare that we wouldn't go home if we could, and the three are Greely Curtis, Henry Higginson and myself. Our tents and the regimental lines have become our homes....

I've all along told you, you ought to remain in London, and I say so still; for that is your post and, pleasant or unpleasant there you should remain. I have told you all along, however, that I didn't like the tone of your letters. Your mind has become morbid and is in a bad way—for yourself—both for the *mens sana* and *corpus sanum*. A year of this life would be most advantageous. Your mind might rest and your body would harden. My advice to you is to wait until you can honorably leave your post and then make a bolt into the wilderness, go to sea before the mast, volunteer for a campaign in Italy, or do anything singularly foolish and exposing you to uncalled for hardship. You may think my advice absurd and never return to it again. I tell you I know you and I have tried the experiment on myself, and I here suggest what you most need, and what you will never be a man without. If you joined an expedition to the North pole you might not discover that *terra incognita*, but you would discover many facts about yourself which would amply repay you the trouble you had had. All a man's life is not meant for books, or for travel in Europe. Turn round and give a year to something new, such as I have suggested, and if you are thought singular you will find yourself wise.

Tuesday, 26th. I suppose you in London think it strange that I do not oftener refer to the war in my letters and discuss movements. The truth is that you probably know far more of what is going on than I do, who rarely see papers, still more rarely go beyond the regimental lines and almost never meet any one possessed of any reliable information. As a rule, so far as my knowledge goes, the letters of correspondents of the press are very delusive. They get their information from newspaper generals and their staffs and rarely tell what they see. Now and then, very rarely, I see a plain, true, outspoken letter of an evident eyewitness....

I have given up philosophising and do not often, except in very muddy weather indulge in lamentation. I think indeed you in London will all bear witness that my letters, under tolerably adverse circumstances, have been reasonably cheerful, and I hope they will remain so, even if the days become blacker than these blackest days I ever saw. We all feel that we are right and that being right, there is for us good in this plan of Providence, if our philosophy could but find it out. Do you remember the first lines of the last chorus in *Samson Agonistes?* They begin, "Though we oft doubt," and I have often tried to recall them lately, but cannot get them all. I hope to live to see the philosophy of this struggle, and see the day when the Lord "will to his faithful servant in his place, bear witness gloriously." Meanwhile, if it is your place to wield the pen, to my no small astonishment I find the sword becoming my weapon and, each in his place, we are working off our shares of the coil. Let us try to do it in our several ways to the best of our ability and uncomplainingly receive whatever fate betides us.

Source: [CAL-1]

∽

APPOINTING GENERAL HOOKER: *"Beware of rashness"*

President Abraham Lincoln
Executive Mansion
Washington, D.C.
January 26, 1863

To Major General Joseph Hooker

General:—

I have placed you at the head of the Army of the Potomac. Of course I have done this upon what appear to me to be sufficient reasons. And yet I think it best for you to know that there are some things in regard to which, I am not quite satisfied with you. I believe you to be a brave and a skillful soldier, which, of course, I like. I also believe you do not mix politics with your profession, in which you are right. You have confidence in yourself, which is a valuable, if not an indispensable quality. You are ambitious, which, within reasonable bounds, does good rather than harm. But I think that during Gen. Burnside's command of the Army, you have taken counsel of your ambition, and thwarted him as much as you could, in which you did a great wrong to the country, and to a most meritorious and honorable brother officer. I have heard, in such way as to believe it, of your recently saying that both the Army and the Government needed a Dictator. Of course it was not for this, but in spite of it, that I have given you the

Quiet on the Picket Line.

command. Only those generals who gain successes, can set up dictators. What I now ask of you is military success, and I will risk the dictatorship. The government will support you to the utmost of its ability, which is neither more nor less than it has done and will do for all commanders. I much fear that the spirit which you have aided to infuse into the Army, of criticizing their Commander, and withholding confidence from him, will now turn upon you. I shall assist you as far as I can, to put it down. Neither you, nor Napoleon, if he were alive again, could get any good out of an army, while such a spirit prevails in it. And now, beware of rashness. Beware of rashness, but with energy, and sleepless vigilance, go forward, and give us victories.

Yours very truly,
A. LINCOLN

Rereading this letter in the presence of Noah Brooks, a journalist, Hooker remarked: "The President is mistaken. I never thwarted Burnside in any way, shape, or manner. Burnside was preeminently a man of deportment: he fought the battle of Fredericksburg on his deportment; he was defeated on his deportment; and he took his

deportment with him out of the Army of the Potomac, thank God!"
When he reread the end of the letter, Hooker said, "That is just such
a letter as a father might write to his son. It is a beautiful letter,
and, although I think he was harder on me than I deserved, I will
say that I love the man who wrote it." (The Century Illustrated
Monthly Magazine, *Volume 49.) President Lincoln relieved Hooker*
(1814–1879) of his command of the Army of the Potomac in late
June, just before the Battle of Gettysburg, which his successor, George
Meade, won.

Source: [AL]

∽

WINTER IN THE SOUTH: *"Here, moreover, are snuff-eating women"*

Sergeant John Whipple, U.S.A.
92nd Regiment, New York State Volunteers
Camp Near New Bern, North Carolina
February 11, 1863

[To _____]

As my motto is "business before pleasure," I will say, first, that
I received a letter from his wife, but C. C. did not, and he begins
to think the Cooper family are all dead or married, or some other
awful thing has happened to them.

We are still at work at our fort. When all is finished we shall be
happy to see our Secesh friends, and would most assuredly give
them a warm reception. The weather is now warm, but a few days
ago we had a snow-storm, and we had no fire in many of our tents,
and were put to our wits' end to keep warm through the night,
and fain would have done it by lying spoon-fashion; but in spite of
ourselves we kept just cool enough to prevent much sleeping. My
sweet potatoes froze; meat shared the same fate, as likewise the
water in our canteens.

The next night we dug holes in our tents, and filling them with
coals, slept as warm as biscuits in an oven.

Do tell them to write, for C. is too good a soldier to be forgotten by anybody. You in your pleasant homes, surrounded by the comforts of life, enjoying the society of friends and relatives, have but a faint idea of the joy a soldier experiences on receiving letters from the loved ones at home. Even if he knows they are all well, he is not satisfied unless he hears directly from their own hand.

Now that the weather has moderated, the dogs lie around the farmhouses basking in the sun, the flies are buzzing, the robins are singing, and after a brisk walk of a mile, one will get under a shade-tree for comfort. And now, all through the pleasant moonlight nights, the frogs croak and whistle the same old monotonous songs their brethren have so often chanted in my ear on the banks of the old Oswegatchie. But the banks of the Neuse differ greatly from those of the Oswegatchie. On the Neuse you find our ox-teams, the animal being hitched as a horse is hitched to a buggy, and is driven by a stick or by reins attached to his horns.

Here, moreover, are snuff-eating women, who take a small stick and pound or chew the end till it gets broomed, then wetting it in their mouth, put it into a box of snuff, and fall to eating and sucking it again and again, passing the snuff-box around like the old ladies of the North, only twice as often. While engaged in this delightful occupation the stick is seen protruding from their mouths three to five inches, causing the ladies to assume a very grotesque and highly interesting appearance, strikingly reminding me of the first lessons given to calves in the art of drinking by inserting a finger in their mouths. I should hardly have believed this if I had not seen it with my own eyes, and known by actual inspection that it was real snuff. It is just as common to see a young lady with her snuff-stick in her mouth here as it is to see one with knitting-work up in Yankeeland. In addition to those things on the banks of the Neuse, are sweet potatoes, which are selling at eighty cents per bushel. Such potatoes I never saw before. They are good boiled, roasted, or fried, and today I bought a sweet-potato pie; it is very skillfully made from the raw material by the good housewives of Craven County, wherein we now do sojourn.

Your humble servant pronounces the potato almost equal to

the pumpkin pie, resembling it in color and taste. Over across the Neuse, in the goodly town of New Bern, where "officers love to congregate," oysters most do flourish and rejoice in her marketplace; and many a broad grin of satisfaction illumines the countenance of the oyster-loving soldier as he pays his "quarter" for a fresh quart, or buys a whole bushel of them in the shell for fifty cents. But "there is a cobweb in every corner;" for although potatoes and oysters are plenty and cheap, everything else is very dear. Poor envelopes sell at twenty cents a bunch, white chalk at twenty cents per pound, eggs twenty-five cents per dozen—and that in this warm country, where hens lay all the year round if they would. No butter or cheese is made here to sell, and but very few of the farmers make enough for their own use. Here are found large tracts of pine, from which our lean, lank, sallow, butternut-dressed Southern brethren obtain their pitch, tar, and turpentine. They first box the trees as some people do the sugar-maple, by cutting a hole in the side that will hold about one quart. Then they proceed to scratch the tree above the box, and the pitch runs down and fills it in about three weeks. As they box seven or eight thousand trees in one lot, they manage to get a large quantity of pitch, which they sell at from five to eight dollars per barrel, according to the demand in market. After running about four months it stops, and what dries and hardens on the trees is scraped off and sold with the rest. Each year they scratch a little higher up the trees; many are cut as high as forty feet or more, and have been tapped at least twenty years. As you may suppose, we of the Ninety-second have plenty of gum to chew, and all the fat pine we want for firewood. Thus you see how pine-sugar (as we call it) is manufactured in this portion of Uncle Sam's vineyard.

But I must tell you of another thing very common on the banks of the Neuse, which you do not enjoy at home, i. e., "picket firing."

Last week, Captain Whitford's guerrillas came down, and getting in the rear of our outpost, fired on our boys, wounding four of them slightly. The pickets, being taken by surprise by being attacked in the rear instead of front, had time to fire but one volley into the rebels before they were in the woods out of sight. Today, our quartermaster and their officer, riding beyond the lines, came unexpectedly upon a body of guerrillas, but by dint of good riding managed to run away unhurt. When they reached the reserve, the old pickets were turned out to deploy as skirmishers through the woods in pursuit. But the rebels had too much the start, and we only got one shot at them, capturing one haversack and canteen. Court Cooper was out, and managed to get one shot at them, and brought in a "johnny-cake" from a secesh haversack. He is going to send a piece home, so look out for rebel rations.

You must know that any alarm on the outpost is the signal for every man in the regiment to fall in. It would do you good to see the Ninety-second on such occasions. When the firing commenced today, I was out with a fatigue party cutting brush, and when the long-roll sounded, such a getting over brush and briers you never did see, for we had to go to camp on the double-quick. As it is natural for me, when anything ridiculous occurs, I had to indulge in a hearty laugh, and more than usual at this time, to see the way they tumbled over the brush in their great haste to get their guns. I had ten men in my squad, and verily I thought some of them would break their necks before reaching camp. We knew perfectly well that there would be no great fighting, but we knew just as well that the long-roll means every man at his post, and orders must be obeyed. I must not write much longer, for a certain gun hanging in the tent needs cleaning, and who will do it if I do not? So, leaving picket-firing, pine-sugar, sweet potatoes, and snuff-eating girls to take care of themselves, I will bring my letter to a close by sending you all the love that such a letter is supposed capable of containing. I remain, as in duty bound, your obedient servant.

Source: [SL]

~

H. H. Penniman, M.D., U.S.A.
Logan's Division, 17th Army Corps
Lake Providence, Louisiana
[February–March] 1863

[To ____]

First we have the drums and fife, ten each to a regiment, at one hour before daylight; and as the regiments do not all commence at the same time, we hear plenty of music early. This is to call the soldiers out in line-of-battle to answer the roll-calls; then they turn in again. The bugles sound at half-past eight in the evening to retire, put out lights, and turn in until morning, when all the music is repeated. It sounds finely at night. At daybreak we have "sick-call" repeated through all the regiments. Two or three drummers and filers stand in front of the "music tent," which is in the center rear, and play an odd piece for three or four minutes; and it seems to say, "Come out, ye sick." This time *we* have to be on hand. The orderlies bring in the sick-list in each company, and such as are able come out. I take the book, call the names, and examine the men; feel of their pulse, look at their tongues, hear

A Morning Lesson

their story, ask questions, make a prescription, and mark their names *excused*, if really sick; if not, *duty* opposite; and those who need medicine step to my assistant or druggist, get the medicine, and leave. I do not get *fooled* very often. You must know if some can get excused, it saves going out on "picket duty" and standing guard nights. I feel sorry for the poor fellows sometimes. When it rains, and I find they are not well enough to bear fatigue and exposure, I favor them all I can; but not one overworks himself. The "sick-call" examinations last half an hour. If any are too sick to come up with the orderly, I go and see them at their quarters after breakfast.

Next we go to breakfast; and then there is the beating of the orderlies' call; then another for the pickets, and so on until nine or ten o'clock: but, except the "sick-call," the medical department give little or no attention to the others. There is the officers' call to dinner, supper, etc., all in music. Once a week there is a general inspection of arms. Our regimental commander, Major Peets, tries to enforce discipline. He had, last week, four men tied by their hands up to a limb of a tree in camp, all day, for stealing. Our regiment has eight new drums; they are about fifty yards from my tent, in the rear of the regiment; and I can tell you I often wish I could put cotton in my ears, especially when they begin to roll out the noise at daybreak—about *twenty* bands of music, fifes and drums. The little fellow in our regiment that beats the bass-drum thumps away as if he expected the others would drown him down, and he is determined to be heard.

You would laugh to see the excitement when the mail arrives. It goes to the division headquarters, and is assorted for different regiments; then it is sent round to the adjutant of each regiment. The way we know of its arrival is, a man with a drum steps out before the adjutant's tent and gives the call for the orderlies. This call is a short prelude or roll and four separate taps of the drum; and moderately the orderly of each company goes to the door and receives the mail for his company: he takes it to the tent of his company and calls out, "Boys, come out for your mail," and then comes a rush!

Source: [SL]

∾

108

CONSCIENCE: *"Can you blame the woman for her tears, secesh though she was?"*

Sergeant John Whipple, U.S.A.
92nd Regiment, New York State Volunteers
Fort Anderson, Maryland
April 14, 1863

[To _____]

Slowly the rain is falling, yet not steadily, and the wind blows by in fitful gusts. The night is very dark, and again I am alone. My partner is on picket duty, and I, seated in my camp, am writing to the "old folks at home." My candle is supported in a quart cup by the last week's "Herald" pressed tightly around it. I have no news of consequence to write, for all is quiet. The "expedition" I referred to in my last returned without accomplishing anything, and today another has gone out to act in concert with one from another quarter, for the relief of Washington. Meanwhile the 92nd "pursues the even tenor of its way," for with *us* "spades are trumps." We do nothing but dig, except guard duty, and we are not desirous of change; for as long as we stay here we can have things comfortable, and live about as easy as at home, excepting picket duty in wet weather.

In your last letter you advise me to come home. I should like very much to act upon your suggestion, but just at the present time I do not think it possible to do so. As for "playing off," as we call it, to get a discharge, I beg leave to assure you the time for that *will never come!* For if I could deceive man, I could not deceive my own conscience. I am coming home as honorable as I left it, or not at all. It is not the whole of life to live in this state of being, for when this world's night shall have passed away with all its darkness, its troubled dreams, its baseless visions, and we wake in the light of an eternal day, may we be spared the thought that *our* part in life's great struggle was not well played; therefore let us not be weary in well-doing. To you at the North, it doubtless seems the very height of trouble to be separated from your relations, children, and friends, knowing they are exposed to dangers and perils at all times; and yet *you* know but little of the miseries of war, compared with those who live in its very midst. If you could

109

" Used Up."

once see the country after an army has passed through it, you would be much more thankful than you are that you live in a land of peace. Only a few days since, our troops burned a widow's house and all the out-buildings, simply because she was *suspected* to be a spy! At times the rebel army marching through a neighborhood will take whatever they like; then *our* army follows, and takes the rest. What would you think to see men come into your farmyard and catch your hens, milk your cows, shoot your pigs, and then make a fire of your garden fence to cook them; and not having the fear of the owner in their minds, upset beehives and carry off the honey?

A few days since, I was on an outpost, near the house of a citizen within our lines, who had just got a pass of the colonel, giving him permission to move his family and effects outside; in case of an attack, his house would probably be destroyed. The woman told me, with tears in her eyes, that she had lived there thirty years, with her husband, and that she herself was born and brought up there. They had determined to stick by, at all hazards; but our troops having planted a battery a few rods from the house the night before, to sweep the road in front of it, in case of an attack, their courage failed them, and they concluded to leave; and so the cart was brought up, and with many a tear and sigh, was loaded for the journey! It was the Sabbath morning, and as quiet, calm, and beautiful a day as ever dawned on the earth. We were far from the bustle and noise of the camp, and naught broke the peaceful stillness of the scene; the bees were humming in the bright sun, the leaves of the apple-tree were starting into life, the blossoms of the peach shook in the breeze, and the garden vegetables were flourishing luxuriantly; and yet, it must be *all* given up, the dear old moss-grown homestead, the valued possessions, and all the associations of a lifetime must be relinquished! Can you blame the woman for her tears, secesh though she was? I really pitied her; for, in all probability, when they return, again to their old home, it will long have been laid in ashes! No neighbors were gathered there to bid them farewell, or assist them in their labors; for no one could come without a pass: only one old lady, who had been to town, stopped there awhile. The old man wished to give her some articles he could not take away, but was afraid to do so without orders, and the old lady was equally perplexed, for although she wanted the articles in question, she had no "creatur" to carry them, and she was too old to "tote 'em" herself, and "reckoned" if she got outside the lines, she "couldn't" get in again without a new pass.

Having charge of the post, and feeling sorry for the old woman, I told her to go for a cart and I would let her in when she came back: so off she started, and went *three miles;* getting a boy and a "creatur," she returned rejoicing. I told the old man he might give her whatever property he saw fit, and I would pass her out; for which he thanked me very much, and proceeded to put a "right smart load" on the cart, till the old lady "reckoned" she had got on all the "creatur" could "tote;" and he reckoning in the same manner, concluded she had got load enough, and then with protestations of love and friendship, and with hopes of better days to come, the old neighbors, with trembling voices, and tears coursing down their cheeks, bade each other good-by! When the cart and its big bundles, and the boy with the broad-brimmed hat, and the old lady with her flaxen hair and long-caped bonnet, and the sorrel "creatur" with its long switched-tail and flowing mane, were lost to sight among the solemn old pines, I sat me down in the pleasant sunshine, and throwing my gun across my lap, mused long on these trying vicissitudes, and the glory of war.

But I have preached enough, and, fearing lest my audience become weary, will even close, wishing you all success, with love to each and all.

Source: [SL]

~

PROPOSAL: *"make certain the comfort that if I should fall I shall fall as your husband"*

Brigadier General George E. Pickett, C.S.A.
In Camp
April 15, 1863

To His Fiancee, La Salle (Sally) Corbell

This morning I awakened from a beautiful dream, and while its glory still overshadows the waking and fills my soul with radiance I write to make an earnest request—entreating, praying, that you will grant it. You know, my darling, we have no prophets in these days to tell us how near or how far is the end of this awful struggle. If "the battle is not to the strong" then we may win; but when all our ports are closed and the world is against us, when for us a man killed is a man lost, while Grant may have twenty-five of every nation to replace one of his, it seems that the battle is to the strong. So often already has hope been dashed to the winds.

Why, dear, only a little while since, the Army of the Potomac recrossed the Rappahannock, defeated, broken in spirit, the men deserting, the subordinate officers so severe in their criticism of their superiors that the great Commander-in-Chief of the Army, Mr. Lincoln, felt it incumbent upon him to write a severe letter of censure and rebuke. Note the change and hear their bugle-call of hope. Hooker, who is alleged to have "the finest army on the planet," is reported to be on the eve of moving against Richmond. My division and that of Hood, together with the artillery of

Dearing and Henry, have been ordered to a point near Petersburg to meet this possible movement.

Now, my darling, may angels guide my pen and help me to write—help me to voice this longing desire of my heart and intercede for me with you for a speedy fulfillment of your promise to be my wife. As you know, it is imperative that I should remain at my post and absolutely impossible for me to come for you. So you will have to come to me. Will you, dear? Will you come? Can't your beautiful eyes see beyond the mist of my eagerness and anxiety that in the bewilderment of my worship—worshiping, as I do, one so divinely right, and feeling that my love is returned—how hard it is for me to ask you to overlook old-time customs, remembering only that you are to be a soldier's wife? A week, a day, an hour as your husband would engulf in its great joy all my past woes and ameliorate all future fears.

So, my Sally, don't let's wait; send me a line back by Jackerie saying you will come. Come at once, my darling, into this valley of the shadow of uncertainty, and make certain the comfort that if I should fall I shall fall as your husband.

You know that I love you with a devotion that absorbs all else—a devotion so divine that when in dreams I see you it is as

something too pure and sacred for mortal touch. And if you only knew the heavenly life which thrills me through when I make it real to myself that you love me, you would understand. Think, my dear little one, of the uncertainty and dangers of even a day of separation, and don't let the time come when either of us will look back and say, "It might have been."

If I am spared, my dear, all my life shall be devoted to making you happy, to keeping all that would hurt you far from you, to making all that is good come near to you. Heaven will help me to be ever helpful to you and will bless me to bless you. If you knew how every hour I kneel at your altar, if you could hear the prayers I offer to you and to our Heavenly Father for you, if you knew the incessant thought and longing and desire to make you blessed, you would know how much your answer will mean to me and how, while I plead, I am held back by a reverence and a sensitive adoration for you. For, my Sally, you are my goddess and I am only

Your devoted,
SOLDIER

Pickett (1825–1875) married Corbell (1843–1931) on September 15, 1863.

Source: [GEP]

CHANCELLORSVILLE: *"I should have chosen for the good of the country to have been disabled in your stead"*

General Robert E. Lee, C.S.A.
Commander, Army of Northern Virginia
Chancellorsville, Virginia
May 4, 1863

To Lieutenant General Thomas J. (Stonewall) Jackson
General:
I have just received your note informing me that you were wounded. I cannot express my regret at the occurrence.
Could I have directed events, I should have chosen for the

good of the country to have been disabled in your stead. I congratulate you upon the victory which is due to your skill and energy.

> Most truly yours,
> R. E. Lee
> General

Chancellorsville was indeed a great victory for the Army of Northern Virginia, but the wounded Jackson died of pneumonia on May 10.

Source: [WJT]

~

Raiding Missouri: *"I never wanted to see you half as bad in all my life as I do now"*

J. C. Morris, C.S.A.
Camp Near Lanjer, Arkansas
May 10, 1863

To His Wife

My Dear Amanda,

It has been a long time since I had an opportunity of writing to you, and I gladly avail myself of the present opportunity. I am not certain that I will have a chance of sending this but I will write a few lines anyhow and try and get it off to let you know that I am among the living.

We have been on a raid into Missouri but I have not time to give you the particulars of our trip. I will write in a few days if I can get a chance to send it and write you a long one. I just came off of picket and found the boys all writing to send by a man that has been discharged who is going to start home this morning. I was quite sick three or four days while in Missouri but have entirely recovered. We captured a good many prisoners while in Mo. and killed a good many. We went up as high as Jackson 8 or 10 miles above Cape Girardeau. We fought them nearly all day

at the Cape on Sunday two weeks ago today. The yanks boasted
that we would never get back to Ark but they were badly mistaken,
for we are back again and have sustained but very light loss, we
never lost a man out of our company and only one or two out of
the regiment. I wish I had time to give you a full description of
our trip. It would be very interesting to you I know; but you will
have to put up with this little scrawl for the present. I am in hopes
that I will get a whole package of letters from you in a few days.
I never wanted to see you half as bad in all my life as I do now.
I would give anything in the world to see you and the children. I
have no idea when I will have that pleasure. We can't get any
news here—do not know what is going on in the outside world.
The boys will all write as soon as they get a chance to send
them off.

We will remain in this vicinity, I expect for some time to recruit
our horses. Our horses are sadly worsted. We found plenty to eat
and to feed our horses on in Mo but hardly even had time to feed
or eat as we traveled almost incessantly night and day. We could
get any amount of bacon of the very best kind at 10 cents and every
thing else in proportion.

I must close for fear I do not get to send my letter off. Write
often. I will get them some time. I will write every chance, do not
be uneasy when you do not get letters, for when we are scouting
around as we have been it is impossible to write or to send them off
if we did write. Give my love to the old Lady and all the friends.
My love and a thousand kisses to my own sweet Amanda and our

little boys. How my heart yearns for thou that are so near and dear to me. Goodbye my own sweet wife, for the present.

As ever your devoted and loving Husband,
J. C. MORRIS

Source: [LL] http://spec.lib.vt.edu/cwlove/jcmorris.html

～

CAVALRY HORSES: *"a horse must go until he can't be spurred any further"*

Captain Charles Francis Adams, Jr.
Camp of First Massachusetts Volunteer Cavalry
Potomac Creek, Virginia
May 12, 1863

To His Mother, Abigail Brown Brooks Adams

It is by no means a pleasant thought to reflect how little people at home know of the non-fighting details of waste and suffering of war. We were in the field four weeks, and only once did I see the enemy, even at a distance. You read of Stoneman's and Grierson's cavalry raids, and of the dashing celerity of their movements and their long, rapid marches. Do you know how cavalry moves? It never goes out of a walk, and four miles an hour is very rapid marching—"killing to horses" as we always describe it. To cover forty miles is nearly fifteen hours march. The suffering is trifling for the men and they are always well in the field in spite of wet and cold and heat, loss of sleep and sleeping on the ground. In the field we have no sickness; when we get into camp it begins to appear at once.

But with the horses it is otherwise and you have no idea of their sufferings. An officer of cavalry needs to be more horse-doctor than soldier, and no one who has not tried it can realize the discouragement to Company commanders in these long and continuous marches. You are a slave to your horses, you work like a dog yourself, and you exact the most extreme care from your Sergeants, and you see diseases creeping on you day by day and your horses breaking down under your eyes, and you have two

resources, one to send them to the reserve camps at the rear and
so strip yourself of your command, and the other to force them
on until they drop and then run for luck that you will be able to
steal horses to remount your men, and keep up the strength of
your command. The last course is the one I adopt. I do my best for
my horses and am sorry for them; but all war is cruel and it is my
business to bring every man I can into the presence of the enemy,
and so make war short.

So I have but one rule, a horse must go until he can't be spurred
any further, and then the rider must get another horse as soon as
he can seize on one. To estimate the wear and tear on horseflesh
you must bear in mind that, in the service in this country, a cavalry
horse when loaded carries an average of 225 lbs. on his back. His
saddle, when packed and without a rider in it, weighs not less
than fifty pounds. The horse is, in active campaign, saddled on
an average about fifteen hours out of the twenty four. His feed is
nominally ten pounds of grain a day and, in reality, he averages
about eight pounds. He has no hay and only such other feed as
he can pick up during halts. The usual water he drinks is brook

water, so muddy by the passage of the column as to be of the color of chocolate. Of course, sore backs are our greatest trouble. Backs soon get feverish under the saddle and the first day's march swells them; after that day by day the trouble grows. No care can stop it. Every night after a march, no matter how late it may be, or tired or hungry I am, if permission is given to unsaddle, I examine all the horses' backs myself and see that everything is done for them that can be done, and yet with every care the marching of the last four weeks disabled ten of my horses, and put ten more on the high road to disability, and this out of sixty—one horse in three.

Imagine a horse with his withers swollen to three times the natural size, and with a volcanic, running sore pouring matter down each side, and you have a case with which every cavalry officer is daily called upon to deal, and you imagine a horse which has still to be ridden until he lays down in sheer suffering under the saddle. Then we seize the first horse we come to and put the dismounted man on his back. The air of Virginia is literally burdened today with the stench of dead horses, federal and confederate. You pass them on every road and find them in every field, while from their carrions you can follow the march of every army that moves.

On this last raid dying horses lined the road on which Stoneman's divisions had passed, and we marched over a road made pestilent by the dead horses of the vanished rebels. Poor brutes! How it would astonish and terrify you and all others at home with your sleek well-fed animals, to see the weak, gaunt, rough animals, with each rib visible and the hip-bones starting through the flesh, on which these "dashing cavalry raids" were executed. It would knock the romance out of you. So much for my cares as a horsemaster, and they are the cares of all. For, I can safely assure you, my horses are not the worst in the regiment and that I am reputed no unsuccessful chief-groom. I put seventy horses in the field on the 13th of April, and not many other Captains in the service did as much. . . .

The present great difficulty is to account for our failure to win a great victory and to destroy the rebel army in the recent battle. They do say that Hooker got frightened and, after Sedgwick's disaster, seemed utterly to lose the capacity for command—he was panic-stricken. Two-thirds of his army had not been engaged at all, and he had not heard from Stoneman, but he was haunted with a vague phantom of danger on his right flank and base, a danger purely of his own imagining, and he had no peace until he found himself on this side of the river. Had he fought his army as he might have fought it, the rebel army would have been destroyed and Richmond today in our possession. We want no more changes, however, in our commanders, and the voice of the Army, I am sure, is to keep Hooker; but I am confident that he is the least respectable and reliable and I fear the least able commander we have had. I never saw him to speak to, but I think him a noisy, low-toned intriguer, conceited, intellectually "smart," physically brave. Morally, I fear, he is weak; his habits are bad and, as a general in high command, I have lost all confidence in him. But the army is large, brave and experienced. We have many good generals and good troops, and, in spite of Hooker, I think much can be done if we are left alone. Give us no more changes and no new generals!

As for the cavalry, its future is just opening and great names will be won in the cavalry from this day forward. How strangely stupid our generals and Government have been! How slow to learn even from the enemy! Here the war is two years old and throughout it we have heard but one story—that in Virginia cavalry was useless, that the arm was the poorest in the service. Men whom we called generals saw the enemy's cavalry go through and round their armies, cutting their lines of supply and exposing their weakness; and yet not one of these generals could sit down and argue thus: "The enemy's cavalry almost ruin me, and I have only a few miles of base and front, all of which I can guard; but the enemy has here in Virginia thousands of miles of communication; they cannot guard it without so weakening their front that I can crush them; if they do not guard it, every bridge is a weak point and I can starve them by cutting off supplies. My cavalry cannot travel in any direction without crossing a railroad, which the enemy cannot guard and which is an artery of their existence. A rail pulled up is a supply train captured. Give me 25,000 cavalry and I will worry the enemy out of Virginia." None of our generals seem to have had the intelligence to argue thus and so they quietly and as a fixed fact said: "Cavalry cannot be used in Virginia," and this too while Stuart and Lee were playing around them. And so they paralyzed their right arm. Two years have taught them a simple lesson and today it is a recognized fact that 25,000 well appointed cavalry could force the enemy out of Virginia. How slow we are as a people to learn the art of war! Still, we do learn.

But the troubles of the cavalry are by no means over. Hooker, it is said, angrily casting about for some one to blame for his repulse, has, of all men, hit upon Stoneman. Why was not Stoneman earlier? Why did not he take Richmond? And they do say Hooker would deprive him of his command if he dared. Meanwhile, if you follow the newspapers, you must often have read of one Pleasonton and his cavalry. Now Pleasonton is the bete noire of all cavalry officers. Stoneman we believe in. We believe in his judgment, his courage and determination. We know he is ready to shoulder responsibility, that he will take good care of us and won't get us into places from which he can't get us out. Pleasonton also we have served under. He is pure and simple a newspaper humbug. You always see his name in the papers, but to us who have served under him and seen him under fire he is notorious as a bully and toady. He does nothing save with a view to a newspaper paragraph. At Antietam he sent his cavalry into a hell of artillery fire and himself got behind a bank and read a newspaper, and there, when we came back, we all saw him and laughed among ourselves. Yet mean and contemptible as Pleasonton is, he is always in at Head Quarters and now they do say that Hooker wishes to depose Stoneman and hand the command over to Pleasonton. You may imagine our sensations in prospect of the change. Hooker is powerful, but Stoneman is successful. . . .

Source: [CAL-2]

H. H. Penniman, M.D., U.S.A.
17th Regiment Illinois Volunteers
Vicksburg, Mississippi
June 1863

To His Wife

I am now with my regiment, and have had an awful time. After
heavy cannonading, Grant's army undertook to carry the forts in
front of this place on the land-side. Got repulsed at every point,
with piles of dead and wounded, many regiments losing 150 men.
It was an awful day. Our hospitals are filled; surgeons are tolerably
plenty. Our heavy cannon are throwing shells over our heads; but
as we lay in a ravine, we are just now safe.

Vicksburg is one continued pile of hills, and on every hill a fort.
It is very dry and dusty. Captain Cornell and two other captains
in the "Ninety-fifth" were killed. Col. Humphrey, not killed, laid
in a trench concealed till night, was wounded in the leg. It was
useless to attempt to storm such forts. It is likely that cannonading
and siegeing at leisure will be the end of this affair. Both parties
are skilful, and have plenty of powder and shot.

Our little regiment have fired away over 100,000 rifle cartridges
since coming here. The most beautiful sight to us is the bombs
at night. They are a great way off, about four miles, as it is three
miles to the river, and our mortarboats are at the other side. Two
or three are climbing up at once high in the sky, describing, of
course, a great circle towards us, and descend down into the town
with an explosion like the heaviest cannon—indeed there is no
noise round the place so awful and so loud. When they explode
just above the houses, the scene is grand indeed, though they do
the most damage when exploding in the streets or in houses. They
have a fuse that shines all the way up and down, and it looks like
a falling star, but much slower. The bomb weighs 245 pounds,
has a shell or body three inches thick, and powder enough for a
dozen big guns, and it is of the size of a common water-bucket.
This mass of iron descends in its great arch from a height of

Coming into Battery Under Fire

from 1500 to 2000 feet, and when it strikes the earth explodes, opening a hole like a great cellar; or, if it bursts in the air, it throws its great pieces of all shapes, and some of them weighing twenty-five pounds, with a force that kills or crushes what of men and things are in the way. More than a keg of powder is used to load the mortar. No one can stand near at the discharge. A long string pulls the lock, and one can see the flash ten or fifteen seconds before the sound reaches one. And then, if one lived in the city, what an awful suspense as to where it will fall. The people are said to live in caves they have made in side-hills, and hide away.

The shell that is now fired from field-pieces, instead of the old-fashioned ball, is a long cylinder, like a good-sized long melon with the end cut square off; the point is towards the enemy, and at its end is a long percussion cap, as large as a small egg: when this hits any obstacle, it explodes, the fragments being driven with great fury and destruction all around. These pieces will kill a man quick, though more often they make a great hole. I have dressed many a dreadful shell-wound.

The accuracy of their fire is wonderful indeed. They throw (the batteries) a shell a half a mile, and hit a man's head if he keep it up a minute too long above the top of the trench. We are behind Vicksburg, which has its front on the river. Our circle round, resting on the river from right to left, inclosing the town, is some ten miles in extent. They have a perfect circle of forts, one acre in extent each, all round on the highest and best-situated points; besides, they have connection from one to another by means of covered ways—i. e., by deep tracks, cut down so that men cannot be seen in their passages. They are covered or hidden from us only by being down below our shot: a man mounted may be seen moving about these passages, but troops can go six abreast, their heads below, all out of sight. So they can reinforce any fort that needs help; and when we tried to storm the forts, we could not make out more than two hundred or three hundred inside by the officers' glasses, but more than ten times the number were ready to receive us and drive us back from a position where one man is equal to one half-dozen, all hid but his head behind breastworks. Two of our regiments, 8th Ohio and 45th Illinois, moved one night close up to the forts, so close that the rebel cannon could not hurt them; and if any of their men reached over with their small guns, our men stood ready to shoot, with guns all cocked, at any moment. After staying there two days they were withdrawn, as they could not go over or up the works; besides they were in our way, as the batteries endangered them in bursting shell thrown at the fort.

The regiments all have their place or chance every fourth day or night. The batteries thunder away all day, and sometimes all night, so as to hinder the rebels from coming out in force and escaping, which they have attempted two or three times; for we not only want their place, but their army. You may be assured there is sharp practice used on both sides.

Source: [SL]

~

COLORED TROOPS: *"if the raising of colored troops prove such a benefit to the country...I shall thank God a thousand times that I was led to take my share in it"*

Colonel Robert Gould Shaw, U.S.A.
Massachusetts Volunteer Infantry 54th Regiment
Steamer *De Molay*
Off Cape Hatteras, Florida
June 1, 1863

[To _____]

The more I think of the passage of the Fifty-fourth through Boston, the more wonderful it seems to me. Just remember our own doubts and fears, and other people's sneering and pitying remarks, when we began last winter, and then look at the perfect triumph of last Thursday.

We have gone quietly along forming the regiment, and at last left Boston amidst a greater enthusiasm than has been seen since the first three-months troops left for the war. Everyone I saw, from the governor's staff down, had nothing but words of praise for us.

Truly I ought to be thankful; and if the raising of colored troops prove such a benefit to the country, and to the blacks, as many people think it will, I shall thank God a thousand times that I was led to take my share in it.

Robert Gould Shaw (1837–1863) led the first Colored Regiment.

Source: [SL]

∾

VICKSBURG: *"War is a dreadful evil, and the army is a school of bad morals"*

H. H. Penniman, M.D., U.S.A.
17th Regiment Illinois Volunteers
Vicksburg, Mississippi
June 6, 1863

Dear Little Wife—

We still lie here waiting for the fall of Vicksburg, and expect it will be ours in from ten days to two weeks from this. Grant's fine army needs a few weeks of rest very much. Marching and countermarching, fighting, watching, and digging, with hot weather, dry and excessively dusty roads and fields, miserable camping-places on the ground, and great scarcity of water—and what we dig for is unhealthy, with very great excess of noxious chemical compounds—short diet, sleepless nights, dirty clothes, absence of tents, distance of wagons, and much confusion among these countless hills, all have aided in rendering the troops debilitated, and most decidedly uncomfortable. Still, there is less sickness than might be anticipated; but there must be a change soon, or we shall suffer much, as all these are gradually rendering the soldiers weak. Tuckered out will express the state of thousands of officers and men. We will get a long rest when we get this place, and there is great need.

I did not stay at the hospital of our division, as another wanted it, and I was sent back to our regiment. As our surgeon, Doctor L. D. Kellogg, has just returned to our regiment, our medical staff is now full. Kellogg, Tompkins, and Penniman, is the full list. But we will not stay so long, probably. We all sleep in one little tent, eight feet square, and are fortunate in having this, as all tents were ordered to be left at Grand Gulf, even such as had not been left by previous orders at the Bend, sixty miles above. We lay under the side of a sharp hill, and our floor of clay is levelled by digging into the bank; and all sleeping-places are behind these ridges, to be out of range of shot and shell from the rebels, who often kill and wound men beyond us, even a mile out, if they can see them. They use splendid rifles, and best of English ammunition, and fire with incredible accuracy. I have had three bullets scatter the dust near me, in quick succession, while walking over a part of one of our roads exposed to view of these rebels. But I shall not go there again, so do not be alarmed, for I could tell you worse stories than this if I wished to alarm you.

The weather is oppressively hot, but I stand it tolerably well; and have only lost some thirty-five pounds since I left you, mostly within the last six weeks. I am, indeed, quite well, and eat our plain fare, and sleep well, and take things as cool as I can. I have plenty of clothing, and need nothing. Do not suppose I am suffering or sick. God be thanked for all his mercies. Our regiment go on duty every fourth day—that is, at 3 o'clock in the morning. We creep up to the front, and into the rifle-pits of the sharpshooters, and relieve the regiment who have been there for twenty-four hours; and do not leave until just before daylight next morning. I and Tompkins stay at the foot of the hill (a mile from here), about twenty rods behind the troops, and, with our little equipment, wait any casualty that may call for our services. We take out rations and two blankets, and pass our time there; sleep on the ground, and fix up brush and wild cane to keep off the sun. The ground here is full of all sorts of insects; and at night, the

The Cavalry Camp.

bugs are plenty, and fireflies so numerous, that it is constant flash, flash, all around.

Heavy cannon boom over us all day, and occasionally in the night; and our men, in their pits, are shooting all day at any thing like a man's head they can see, or the place from which a little smoke issues from some rebel gun, distance about one thousand feet, over a deep and wide hollow. I will tell you all about these things, when kind Providence brings me to you again. I hope we will be paid some money—and all of us need it—when Vicksburg is taken.

War is a dreadful evil, and the army is a school of bad morals; about nine-tenths of the troops entering the army irreligious, become worse and worse. A great crowd of men, without the restraints of society, and no influence from woman, become very vulgar in language, coarse in their jokes, impious, and almost blasphemous in their profanity. I have never mingled, you know, with the lower dregs of society, and, every day, the associations are painful. It is dreadful and disgusting. Profanity is universal—often, and generally common oaths—sometimes dreadfully severe and heaven-daring in its tone. Such use of the name of the great and ever blessed God, and of the precious Saviour, causes me to feel shocked through and through. I am not squeamish, you know, and not very sensitive, and yet it is awful to hear the cold-blooded insults to God, and the contempt heaped upon the blessed Saviour of the world; and, with few exceptions, rare indeed, among some of superior education and high moral tone, cursing and swearing is common, and very frequent, especially upon the most trifling occasions, and even without any occasion.

This state of impiety will submit to no check nor admonition. The chaplains are of little account, and generally keep regimental post-offices; attend to such light duties, and, so far as I learn, are discouraged in endeavoring to reform abuses. Our regiment has had no chaplain for nearly a year. From all I can learn, his acquaintance had but little or no confidence in his piety. He had no influence; and, indeed, it is in some regiments like going among swine with pearls, and showing the brutes clean garments, to reform their habits. An occasional quiet remark, a question whose name the swearer used, and strict example in all I say and do, is about all I can do. It is dreadful to see how much worse a mess or squad will become after one of their number is killed. We had a fine young man killed out of our hospital mess, as I wrote you, and since that the balance, some nine or ten, are more profane, more trifling, more reckless, more everything that indicates a worse condition of heart, than before.

To pass away time, to play cards, to drink, to eat, to run round, to do anything that will hinder the serious thoughts of eternity, this is all; and of the two persons in our regiment, reputed to be religious, one is not agreeable, and the other I tried in vain to draw into some very general religious talk, the other day, while we were both at leisure up the front: it was no use. Action, not thought; a man had better form his character and principles before he gets into the army.

Drinking is abundant in the army, though this is a luxury denied at these situations except to officers. By liquor time is killed, spirits supported, care dismissed, and thought drowned. Indeed, I had no idea how dreadful are morals in the army. I will explain

these matters to you. Every other man will get drunk if he can, and every officer is frequently drunk. General John A. L——— is stupidly drunk, report says, every night; and officers follow suit, generally. Sabbaths come and go unheeded, no difference; same cannonading, same duties, and all. It is a fact, that the blessed Subbath has passed more than once, and I did not know it. Marching for weeks, fatigued, no books, no almanacs, no papers, baggage all behind, and up and at it again, hasty meals, and nothing to remind us, and not one in a dozen knows the day of the week with certainty. All this is dreadful; but true camp-life is rough and dreadful.

YOUR AFFECTIONATE HUSBAND

Source: [SL]

〰

APPROACH TO GETTYSBURG: *"Our men seem to be in the spirit and feel confident. They laugh at the idea of meeting militia"*

Major General William Dorsey Pender, C.S.A.
Fayetteville, Pennsylvania
June 28, 1863

My dearest Wife—

Our mail came in today and the only thing I heard from you was that four letters had reached Shocco the day after you left. We are resting today after marching 157 miles since leaving Fredericksburg twelve days ago yesterday. If I had any surety that you would get this in a reasonable time, I should have a good deal to tell you.

Until we crossed the Md. line our men behave as well as troops could, but here it will be hard to restrain them, for they have an idea that they are to indulge in unlicensed plunder. They have done nothing like the Yankees do in our country. They take poultry and hogs but in most cases pay our money for it. We take everything we want for government use. The people are frightened to death and will do anything we intimate to them. The rascals have been expecting us and run off most of their stock and goods.

OFF DUTY

I bought a few articles for you yesterday and will get you a nice lot before we leave. We pay about 200 percent.

I am tired of invasions for although they have made us suffer all that people can suffer, I cannot get my resentment to that point to make me feel indifferent to what you see here. But for the demoralizing effect plundering would have on our troops, they would feel war in all its horrors. I never saw people so badly scared. We have only to wish for a thing and it is done. I have made up my mind to enjoy no hospitality or kindness from any of them.

Everything seems to be going finely. We might get to Phila without a fight. I believe, if we should choose to go. Gen. Lee intimates to no one what he is up to, and we can only surmise. I hope we may be in Harrisburg in three days. What a fine commentary upon their 90 days crushing out, if we should march to the Capital of one of their largest states without a blow. It seems to be the impression that Hooker will not leave Washington, but will leave the states to take care of themselves.

We are in Adams Co., having marched through Franklin. If we do not succeed in accomplishing a great deal all of us will be

surprised. Our men seem to be in the spirit and feel confident.
They laugh at the idea of meeting militia. This is a most
magnificent country to look at, but the most miserable people. I
have yet to see a nice looking lady. They are coarse and dirty, and
the number of dirty looking children is perfectly astonishing. A
great many of the women go barefooted and but a small fraction
wear stockings. I hope we may never have such people....Nearly
all of them seem to be tenants and at first I thought all the
better people must have left. And such barns I never dreamt of.
Their dwelling houses are large and comfortable, looking from
the outside—have not been inside—but such coarse louts that
live in them. I really did not believe that there was so much
difference between our ladies and their females. I have seen
no ladies. We passed through Hagerstown...but saw little
Southern feeling displayed. The fact is the people in N.W.
Md. are as much of the Dutch Yankee as these, and I do not
want them. I hope you reached home safely and feel satisfied
with me, and see that this time at least, you did not leave camp
too soon.

I never saw troops march as ours do; they will go 15 or 20 miles a
day without leaving a straggler and hoop and yell on all occasions.
Confidence and good spirits seem to possess everyone. I wish we
could meet Hooker and have the matter settled at once. We got
the Richmond papers of the 24th today and they bring us good
news from Vicksburg. This campaign will do one of two things:
viz—to cause a speedy peace or a more tremendous war than we
have had, the former may God grant.

Joe enters into the invasion with much gusto and is quite active
in looking up hidden property. In fact the negroes seem to have
more feeling in the matter than the white men and have come
to the conclusion that they will impress horses, etc., etc. to any
amount. Columbus is laying in a stock for his sweetheart and
sisters. Gen. Hill thus far has managed the march of his Corps
and I think will give as much satisfaction as Lt. Gen'l as he did as
Maj. Gen'l. My love to all and keep my folks in Edgecombe posted
as to my well being. Write to me occasionally...Now darling, may
our Good Father protect us and preserve us to each other to a good

old age. Tell Turner I have a pretty pair of low patent leather shoes with heels for him.

YOUR LOVING HUSBAND

Pender was wounded at Gettysburg on July 4 and died July 18. On the field, he informed a chaplain, "Tell my wife that I do not fear to die. . . . My only regret is to leave her and our two children." [Hassler, 260]

Source: [WDP]

~

APPROACH TO GETTYSBURG: *"All the fences that are burnt now are Yankee fences"*

Sergeant Iowa Michigan Royster, C.S.A.
37th N.C.G. Lane's Brigade, Pender's Division, Hill's Corps
Chambersburg, Pennsylvania
June 29, 1863

Dear Ma:

I suppose you saw in the "Progress" newspaper a notice of my appointment to this regiment. It was quite unexpected. I had made a request to Capt. Nicholson of this reg't to recommend me to the Col. but he did not expect any good result. When I read the appointment in the newspaper I was under arrest in my old company. In a day or two came a note from Col. Barbour of the 37th asking Col. Baker to send me to him as I had been appointed in his regiment. Col. Baker released me from arrest and sent me on with many expressions of goodwill, and wishes for my future success. The occasion of my arrest was this. Col. Baker gave an order that the first sergeants should call out the men and make them clear out the camp—cut down the trees and pull up the brush. It was Sunday and I was acting as 1st Sergeant of Co. E. I refused to obey the order. I wouldn't make the men work on the Sabbath, and I was ordered to go to my tent and consider myself under arrest. It was less than a week before I heard of my appointment. The reg't had two fights with the Yankees while I was under arrest. I didn't have to fight. They had taken my arms from me and sent me back to the wagon train. So it was a good thing at last.

On my way to join my reg't, I came by Winchester and saw Kate. She had rec'd a letter from you dated in Jan. and was preparing to answer it. She and I are engaged. Tell my Papa that I don't know how much her father is worth.

Don't know whether he is worth anything or not—couldn't come within ten thousand dollars of the amount to save my life. All of his good instructions lost. Well, "a fool will have his own way." Quick courtship, wasn't it? A week's acquaintance last September and two days in June. I congratulate myself on my promptness. Great quality in a soldier. When I left Winchester Kate gave me a bundle of provisions, a paper of candy, raisins, etc., some handkerchiefs, trimmed my hat, and did a great many things to captivate me.

I sold my horse for 350 dollars and my saddle for fifty. So I have 400 cash with me. I wish I could get a chance to send it to Raleigh and settle Mr. Lovejoy's account. I am so extravagant that I am afraid I shall spend all my money here and have none, or if I get knocked over by a Minnie I would not like for the Yankees to get my Confederate.

I am the only officer present in my company. The men are very clever. There is not one among them who swears or uses any profane language. There are about twenty four. When the co. started from N. C. it numbered 126. At Sharpsburg last September only five. The Capt. went back a few days ago on business expecting to join us in a few days. I fear that the Yankees have got him. He is a member of the Baptist Church. When the company was first made up, the captain, the three lieutenants and one private were all preachers. Every regiment in the brigade has a chaplain; I heard a sermon yesterday. In this brigade there are the 18th, 7th, 33rd, and 87th and 28th reg'ts. I find a great many old acquaintances among them, and on the whole have quite a pleasant time. Everybody told me that my feet would be blistered, but I have been marching nearly a week and have experienced no inconvenience, though several men have fallen by the road. There is no straggling. All are compelled to keep up. Those who are too weak or sick ride in ambulances or wagons. Lee has fully double the number of men he had at Sharpsburg. Our regiment for instance had only fifty at Sharpsburg, there about two hundred and seventy five now. The other regiments are the same way.

Yesterday and the day before our soldiers plundered far and wide—taking butter, milk, apple-butter, fruit, chickens, pigs and horses and everything they could lay their hands on. The people are frightened out of their senses. "Take anything you want but don't hurt us!" is their cry. They are afraid to protest against anything. It is the most beautiful country you ever saw, the neatest farms, fine houses, good fences. The whole country is covered with the finest crops of wheat, such wheat as is not seen in our country.

Yesterday however, Gen'l Lee sent an order around that all stealing and plundering should be punished in each case with death, that officers should be held accountable for the execution of his orders, that he made war upon armed men—not upon women and children. The plundering will be stopped now. I never saw people so submissive and badly scared as these people in my life. It must be conscience. They know how their soldiers have desolated Virginia and they fear that ours will retaliate. But I can't bear it. I hate to take anything when it is given from fear. Quartermasters and Commissaries and Surgeons are empowered to impress everything necessary for the use of the army. But men are not allowed to have anything but what they buy.

I heard but don't know how true it is that nine of our soldiers were shot yesterday for taking jewelry from off the persons of the women. The articles of war make a death punishment for stealing, and in an enemy's country a regimental court-martial has the power to inflict this punishment. Gen. Lee seems determined to stop all marauding. I don't know what place we shall attack, most seem to think Harrisburg. For my part I want to stay here until the war is over, and take their towns and beat their armies and live on their people. Lee's men have unbounded confidence in him. The Yankees are in great perplexity—don't know what point to reinforce—don't know whether Lee will attack Harrisburg,

Pittsburgh, Baltimore, or Washington. I want to take them all. It is glorious. All the fences that are burnt now are Yankee fences. They'll be willing for us to stay out of the Union hereafter. We've come back to the Union, but not as they expected. Write soon.

Source: [VS] http://valley.lib.virginia.edu/papers/F4044 {Source copy consulted: Royster Family Papers, #4183, Southern Historical Collection, University of North Carolina, Chapel Hill. Used with permission from Southern Historical Collection, University of North Carolina, Chapel Hill} {Copyright 2002 by the Rector and Visitors of the University of Virginia}

$\approx$

FREED SLAVES: *"Can you imagine anything more wonderful than a colored abolitionist-meeting, on a South Carolina plantation?"*

Colonel Robert Gould Shaw, U.S.A.
Massachusetts Volunteer Infantry 54th Regiment
St. Helena's Island, South Carolina
July 3, 1863

To His Family

You will have been some time without letters from, me, when you receive this, as the *Arago* was not allowed to take a mail last week, I understand, because of the late movement on Charleston. Last evening I went over to tea at a plantation four or five miles from here, where some of the teachers, four ladies, and the same number of gentlemen, live.

After tea, we went to what the negroes call a "praise-meeting," which was very interesting. The praying was done by an old blind fellow, who made believe all the time that he was reading out of a book. He was also the leader in the singing, and seemed to throw his whole soul into it. After the meeting, there was a "shout," which is a most extraordinary performance. They all walk and shuffle round in a ring, singing and chanting, while three or four stand in a corner and clap their hands to mark the time. At certain parts of the chorus, they all give a duck, the effect of which is very peculiar.

This shuffling is what they call "shouting." They sometimes keep it up all night, and only church-members are allowed to join in it.

Their singing, when there are a great many voices, is fine, but otherwise I don't like it at all. The women's voices are so shrill, that I can't listen to them with comfort.

July 4th.—Today there has been a great meeting for the colored people, at the Baptist church, six or seven miles from camp. I rode down there, and heard a speech from a colored preacher, from Baltimore, named Lynch. He was very eloquent.

Can you imagine anything more wonderful than a colored abolitionist-meeting, on a South Carolina plantation? Here were collected all the freed slaves on this island, listening to the most ultra abolition speeches that could be made, while two years ago their masters were still here, the lords of the soil and of them. Now, they all own something themselves, go to school and to church, and work for wages! It is the most extraordinary change. Such things oblige a man to believe that God is not very far off.

A little black boy read the Declaration of Independence, and then they all sang some of their hymns. The effect was grand. I would have given anything to have had you there; I thought of you all the time.

The day was beautiful, and the crowd was collected in the church-yard, under some magnificent old oaks, covered with the long, hanging gray moss which grows on the trees here. The gay dresses and turbans of the women made the sight very brilliant. Miss Forten promised to write me out the words of some of the hymns they sang, which I will send to you.

July 6th.—Yesterday I went to church at the same place, where the meeting was held on the 4th.

The preaching was very bad, being full of "hell and damnation," but administered in such a dull way, that sleep soon overcame most of the congregation, and we counted fifty darkies fast in the "arms of Murphy."

After the sermon, the preacher said, "Those who wish to be married can come forward." Someone then punched a stout young fellow in white gloves, near me; and as soon as he could be roused and made to understand that the hour was come, he walked up to the altar. A young woman, still stouter and broader-shouldered than the bridegroom, advanced from the women's side of the church, accompanied by a friend, and they both stood by his side, so that it looked as if he were being married to both of them. However, they got through it all right, as he evidently knew which was which, and they both said "Yes, sir," to all the preacher asked them; they were both coal-black. I couldn't find out if the bride had been sleeping during the sermon, as well as the groom.

At the church they sang our hymns, and made a sad mess of them, but they do justice to their own at their "praise-meetings."

9 p.m.—We have just had Miss Forten and two other ladies to tea, and entertained them afterwards with some singing from the men. It made us all think of those last evenings at Readville, which were so pleasant.

If there were any certainty of our being permanently here, you and Annie could come down and spend a month without the least difficulty. You would enjoy it immensely; there is enough here to interest you for months.

As you may suppose, I was bitterly disappointed at being left behind; but nothing has been done at Charleston yet, and we may have a chance.

Today I went on board the monitor *Montauk* and the rebel ram *Fingal*. The latter is very strong and very powerfully armed; but the work is rough, and looks as if they wanted money and workmen to finish it properly.

We don't know with any certainty what is going on in the North, but can't believe Lee will get far into Pennsylvania. No matter if the rebels get to New York, I shall never lose my faith in our ultimate success. We are not yet ready for peace, and want a good deal of purging still.

I wrote to General Strong this afternoon, and expressed my wish to be in his brigade. Though I like Montgomery, I want to get my men alongside of white troops, and into a good fight, if there is to be one. The General sent me word, before he went away, that he was very much disappointed at being ordered to leave us; so I thought it well to put it into his head to try to get us back.

Working independently, the colored troops come only under the eyes of their own officers; and to have their worth properly acknowledged, they should be with other troops in action. It is

an incentive to them, too, to do their best. There is some rumor tonight of our being ordered to James Island, and put under General Terry's command. I should be satisfied with that.

Colonel Shaw was killed in the attack on Fort Wagner, South Carolina, on July 18, 1863.

Source: [SL]

~

GETTYSBURG: *"but for you, my darling, he would rather...be back there with his dead, to sleep for all time in an unknown grave"*

General George E. Pickett, C.S.A.
In Camp, Gettysburg, Pennsylvania
July 4, 1863

To His Fiancee, La Salle (Sally) Corbell

My letter of yesterday, my darling, written before the battle, was full of hope and cheer; even though it told you of the long hours of waiting from four in the morning, when Gary's pistol

rang out from the Federal lines signaling the attack upon Culp's
Hill, to the solemn eight-o'clock review of my men, who rose
and stood silently lifting their hats in loving reverence as Marse
Robert, Old Peter and your own Soldier reviewed them—on then
to the deadly stillness of the five hours following, when the men
lay in the tall grass in the rear of the artillery line, the July sun
pouring its scorching rays almost vertically down upon them,
till one o'clock when the awful silence of the vast battlefield was
broken by a cannon-shot which opened the greatest artillery duel
of the world. The firing lasted two hours. When it ceased we took
advantage of the blackened field and in the glowering darkness
formed our attacking column just before the brow of Seminary
Ridge.

I closed my letter to you a little before three o'clock and rode
up to Old Peter [General James Longstreet] for orders. I found
him like a great lion at bay. I have never seen him so grave and
troubled. For several minutes after I had saluted him he looked at
me without speaking. Then in an agonized voice, the reserve all
gone, he said:

"Pickett, I am being crucified at the thought of the sacrifice of life which this attack will make. I have instructed Alexander to watch the effect of our fire upon the enemy, and when it begins to tell he must take the responsibility and give you your orders, for I can't."

While he was yet speaking a note was brought to me from Alexander. After reading it I handed it to him, asking if I should obey and go forward. He looked at me for a moment, then held out his hand. Presently, clasping his other hand over mine without speaking he bowed his head upon his breast. I shall never forget the look in his face nor the clasp of his hand when I said:—"Then, General, I shall lead my Division on." I had ridden only a few paces when I remembered your letter and (forgive me) thoughtlessly scribbled in a corner of the envelope, "If Old Peter's nod means death then good-by and God bless you, little one," turned back and asked the dear old chief if he would be good enough to mail it for me. As he took your letter from me, my darling, I saw tears glistening on his cheeks and beard. The stern old war-horse, God bless him, was weeping for his men and, I know, praying too that this cup might pass from them. I obeyed the silent assent of his bowed head, an assent given against his own convictions,—given in anguish and with reluctance.

My brave boys were full of hope and confident of victory as I led them forth, forming them in column of attack, and though officers and men alike knew what was before them,—knew the odds against them,—they eagerly offered up their lives on the altar of duty, having absolute faith in their ultimate success. Over on Cemetery Ridge the Federals beheld a scene never before witnessed on this continent,—a scene which has never previously been enacted and can never take place again—an army forming in line of battle in full view, under their very eyes—charging across a space nearly a mile in length over fields of waving grain and anon of stubble and then a smooth expanse—moving with the steadiness of a dress parade, the pride and glory soon to be crushed by an overwhelming heartbreak.

Well, it is all over now. The battle is lost, and many of us are prisoners, many are dead, many wounded, bleeding and dying.

Your Soldier lives and mourns and but for you, my darling, he would rather, a million times rather, be back there with his dead, to sleep for all time in an unknown grave.

Your sorrowing
Soldier

Source: [GEP]

~

VICKSBURG: *"I never was so happy in my life over any particular event"*

Sergeant Stephen A. Rollins, U.S.A.
95th Illinois Infantry
"In Vicksburg (not in rear of)"
July 5, 1863

Dear Mother—

The great work has at last been accomplished—the fight is fought, and the victory won! The great rebel stronghold has at last fallen, and let us thank God fervently. Your son has had the unspeakable pleasure of planting with his own hands the "Stars and Stripes" of America upon the strongest fortress of his country's foes! 'Tis a deed that must live with me and help me. 'Twere useless to add, I'm more than proud of it. Thanks be to God first, who has ruled our affairs to the dismay of our enemies! Thanks next to the patriotism, valor, ability, and energy of Major-General U. S. Grant! Thanks to the soldiers, who have nobly and patriotically performed so many deeds of valor, endured so many hardships, and bravely won so many victories! Thanks, also, to the hearty sympathy of the friends at home! The cause is worthy of their most cordial co-operation and earnest support.

Our only regret and sorrow is over the death of our comrades in arms. But they have not died in vain; their deeds will live in history, and their virtues be remembered until the day-star of Time shall have launched into an endless eternity!

Yesterday was a glorious Fourth. It was one that will live. Hereafter the day on which our fathers declared their independence, and threw off the oppressive yoke of England, will be doubly dear to the American heart. The enemy feel as much chagrined as we do joyful, over the fact of the city being surrendered on the 4th of July. Our brigade was one of the three that went into the city to take possession—a mark of honor in appreciation of our meritorious conduct in the siege of the last 46 days. Such marks of honor are highly valued by the soldiers.

I never was so happy in my life over any particular event; I was calmly happy. My feelings could well correspond to the description given by the newly converted sinner of his new-found happiness. Oh, how I longed to fly to the loyal North and communicate the glorious news! This is the severest blow the rebels have received since the commencement of this unholy rebellion. Thank God for it!

The rebels themselves I think do not feel very bad about it. They are the best-looking set of prisoners I have ever seen. They were "starved out"; that is the way we took them.

The munitions of war found in the city are unbounded. Today we move camp into the city. A large force under General Sherman had gone to the rear last night to whip General Johnston: they'll do it too, or Mr. Johnston will skedaddle lively; which I think he will do. I am almost glad the rebs are making a raid in the Eastern States. It will waken them up, which they need very much. I hope the rebs will get all they want, and more too.

Rollins was killed on June 10, 1864, in Guntown, Mississippi.

Source: [SL]

∾

GETTYSBURG: *"I, believing in the promised support, led them on—on—on—Oh, God!"*

General George E. Pickett, C.S.A.
On the Retreat South from Gettyburg
July 6, 1863

To His Fiancee, La Salle (Sally) Corbell

On the Fourth—far from a glorious Fourth to us or to any with love for his fellow-men—I wrote you just a line of heartbreak. The sacrifice of life on that blood-soaked field on the fatal third was too awful for the heralding of victory, even for our victorious foe, who I think, believe as we do, that it decided the fate of our cause. No words can picture the anguish of that roll-call—the breathless waits between the responses. The "Here" of those who, by God's mercy, had miraculously escaped the awful rain of shot and shell was a sob—a gasp—a knell—for the unanswered name of his comrade. There was no tone of thankfulness for having been spared to answer to their names, but rather a toll, and an unvoiced wish that they, too, had been among the missing.

Even now I can hear them cheering as I gave the order, "Forward!" I can feel the thrill of their joyous voices as they called out all along the line, "We'll follow you, Marse George. We'll follow you—we'll follow you." Oh, how faithfully they kept their word—following me on—on—to their death, and I, believing in the promised support, led them on—on—on—Oh, God!

I can't write you a love-letter today, my Sally, for with my great love for you and my gratitude to God for sparing my life to devote to you, comes the overpowering thought of those whose lives were sacrificed—of the broken-hearted widows and mothers and orphans. The moans of my wounded boys, the sight of the dead, upturned faces, flood my soul with grief—and here am I whom they trusted, whom they followed, leaving them on that field of carnage—and guarding four thousand prisoners across the river back to Winchester. Such a duty for men who a few hours ago covered themselves with glory eternal!

Going To Provost Head-Quarters.   Under Guard.

Well, my darling, I put the prisoners all on their honor and gave them equal liberties with my own soldier boys. My first command to them was to go and enjoy themselves the best they could, and they have obeyed my order. Today a Dutchman and two of his comrades came up and told me that they were lost and besought me to help them find their comrades. They had been with my men and were separated from their own comrades. So I sent old Floyd off on St. Paul to find out where they belonged and deliver them.

This is too gloomy and too poor a letter for so beautiful a sweetheart, but it seems sacrilegious, almost, to say I love you, with the hearts that are stilled to love on the field of battle.

YOUR SOLDIER

Source: [GEP]

President Abraham Lincoln
Washington, D.C.
July 13, 1863

To Major General Ulysses S. Grant

My dear General—

I do not remember that you and I ever met personally. I write this now as a grateful acknowledgment for the almost inestimable service you have done the country. I wish to say a word further. When you first reached the vicinity of Vicksburg, I thought you should do, what you finally did—march the troops across the neck, run the batteries with the transports, and thus go below; and I never had any faith, except a general hope that you knew better than I, that the Yazoo Pass expedition, and the like, could succeed. When you got below, and took Port-Gibson, Grand Gulf, and vicinity, I thought you should go down the river and join Gen. Banks; and when you turned Northward East of the Big Black, I feared it was a mistake. I now wish to make the personal acknowledgment that you were right, and I was wrong.

Yours very truly,
A. LINCOLN

Source: [AL]

∾

Emily Bliss Thacher Souder
Gettysburg, Pennsylvania
July 20, 1863

To J. A. Thacher

My Dear Brother:

You will be surprised to receive a letter from me, bearing "Gettysburg" as a postmark. I left home, with a little company of friends, a week ago today, and arrived here after a wearisome journey, via Baltimore, on Tuesday night.

We commenced our labors at once in the field hospital of the Second Corps, to distribute milk punch, prepared from condensed milk, an invaluable thing in the hospitals, and to prepare nourishing food for our wounded soldiers, corn-starch and farina, eggs in various shapes, and nicely made tea and coffee. Each day, as we have opportunity, we visit the soldiers in their tents, and try to speak a word of cheer. I was surprised and much interested to find the Colonel of the First Minnesota, with Lieutenant Mason and several of their regiment, in the same tent. I promised to take them under my especial charge. Colonel Colvill was much pleased to find that I was your sister, and wanted to know if I intended writing to you soon. I will get the names of these Minnesota boys, and send them to you, if possible. I was glad to be able to give to each of them an orange, a luxury much craved and difficult to obtain at this season, and took to them some chicken soup, which they thought very comfortable. I have seen a number of Minnesota boys, but have not their names, and am sorry to add, have seen also the graves of many Minnesotians.

A great many Maine boys are here, especially of the 19th Maine, which was terribly cut up.

We have several times visited the Adjutant of the 17th Maine, a pleasant young man from Portland, who bears the suffering from an amputated limb with great cheerfulness. He is quartered in a private house in the town. On the opposite side of the street is a young captain of the same regiment, who has lost his arm, Captain Young. He was wounded, I believe, in the first day's battle, and like many others laid several days in the woods without attention. The faces of these New England boys light up with pleasure, as they learn that several of our little company are from the East, though now residents of the City of Brotherly Love, and all the soldiers love to hear of Philadelphia.

The beautiful fields around Gettysburg bear painful evidence of the recent struggle. We are very busy every day, and have not attempted to visit any of the various points of interest.

Wednesday morning.—A man named Crowley, of the 1st Minnesota, who enlisted at St. Paul, was breathing his last, when we left the camp last evening. Lieutenant M. will go to Baltimore today. He is an interesting young man, wounded in the hand. It is impossible to remember the names and identity of these soldiers, except in particular instances. We shall probably remain here another week, if we continue reasonably well. Colonel Colvill has several times asked if I had sent my letter to you yet, and desired his regards. I will send it, therefore, without any further delay. The ambulance is waiting for us. Goodbye.

YOUR AFFECTIONATE SISTER

Source: [EBTS]

∾

VICKSBURG CAMPAIGN: *"Don't think so much of me. I am all right"*

Chauncey H. Cooke, U.S.A.
Head Quarters, Wisconsin Regiment
Snyder's Bluff, Mississippi
July 28, 1863

Dear Mother:

Your last letter at hand. There is no medicine like a letter from home. Let me tell you mother it does a fellow a lot of good. I am glad you are having such success with the bees. It makes my mouth water for biscuit and honey. I wish you would not take so many chances of getting stung. You ought to wear a veil of cheese cloth over your face. Don't think so much of me. I am all right. We have a plenty to eat. By paying a good round price we can get almost anything good to eat. I wish you would think more of yourself. When I see you in my sleep working in the hayfield helping to get up the hay it troubles me. I suppose as you say that help is hard to get and maybe there is no other way. I am careful you may be sure what I eat. Our dainties we get of the sutler, and it is nearly all in cans. I eat a lot of oysters and I find them good for me. That deer that father killed must have come in good play. Don't spoil your relish for it by constantly thinking of me. I told you I am all right. When I get a dish of oysters I always think how fond father is of them.

You say they are going to get rich in Bennet Valley where father bought that forty for me. Well I am happy to know that. It may be they will have use for a part of it when the next recruiting officer comes that way. Nor will he, likely as not, waste his eloquence in trying to coax them to enlist as J. A. Brackett did when I enlisted. He will like as not tell them to furnish so many men or stand a draft.

This war ain't over yet. There may be a lot of money paid out for substitutes yet. Just think of it, they are paying as high as a thousand dollars for substitutes in many of the states. It all means that people are getting tired of the fussy way the war is being carried on. If the slaves had been declared free right at the start, just as father said, and put into the ranks to fight, the war might have ended long ago. I see by the papers there are fifty thousand freedmen under arms and they are doing good service. The poor black devils are fighting for their wives and children, yes and for their lives, while we white cusses are fighting for what Capt. Dorwin calls an idea. I tell the boys right to their face I am in the war for the freedom of the slave. When they talk about the saving of the Union I tell them that is Dutch to me. I am for helping the slaves if the Union goes to smash. Most of the boys have their laugh at me for helping the "Niggers" but Elder Harwood and Ed. Coleman and Julius Parr and Joel Harmon and Chet Ide, the last two of Mondovi, tell me I am right in my argument.

I am sorry father lost that deer. He should take old Prince to help him next time. It is too bad to wound a deer for the wolves to

catch and eat up in that way. We have fresh beef all the time since the surrender. These canebrakes are full of halfwild cattle, and they are fat as butter.

I thank brother W. for sending me those stamps. I will send him a book when I get to Memphis. Mother, I wish you would send me a small package of butter by Lieut. McKay, who is home on furlough for thirty days. I like John McKay. He is a good man. He is a good officer and fair to his men. His wife, I think, is in Modena, where he enlisted. You will see a notice of his arrival in the Alma Journal. For the can of butter you send I want you to reserve a ten-dollar greenback for your own especial use out of the sum I send you. Goodbye, dear mother.

Your boy,
CHAUNCEY

Source: [WMH]

RECEIVING LETTERS: *"to get into camp at last and hear that a mail has come!"*

Captain Charles Francis Adams, Jr., U.S.A.
Camp of First Massachusetts Cavalry
Amissville, Virginia
August 2, 1863

To His Brother, Henry Adams

Your letters have reached me of late slowly, but tolerably surely and you cannot imagine how welcome they have been. John is the only person on this side of the water who ever writes to me now, and he is not very regular. Lou has not written me a line since the 1st of May. Of course I well know that writing to me now is a labor of love and a decidedly unequal bargain, for I have neither time nor conveniences to do my share in a correspondence; but on the other hand letters are more than ever before prized by me, for now they constitute absolutely my only link with the world and my own past, and moreover my only pleasure.

After long marches and great exposure, when you have been forced to drag your tired body up onto your tired horse day after day; when you have been hungry, thirsty and tired, and after breakfasting before sunrise have gone supperless to sleep in a rain storm long after night; when you have gone through all that man can go through, except the worst of all sufferings—cold—then to get into camp at last and hear that a mail has come! People at home don't know what it is. You should see the news fly round the camp and the men's faces light up, and how duty, discipline, everything, at once gives way to the reading of the letters. It's like fresh water in an August noon; and yet of all my family and friends you in London, and now and then John, are the only living souls who ever do more than just answer my letters to them. But you are all models of thoughtfulness in this respect and, while you will never know how much pleasure your letters have given me, I can never express to you how much their regularity has touched and gratified me.

Source: [CAL-2]

A Proffered Resignation: *"The general remedy for the want of success in a military commander is his removal"*

General Robert E. Lee, C.S.A.
Commander of the Army of Northern Virginia
Camp Orange, Virginia
August 5, 1863

To Confederate President Jefferson Davis

Mr. President:

Your letters of the 28th of July and 2nd of August have been received, and I have waited for a leisure hour to reply, but I fear that will never come. I am extremely obliged to you for the attention given to the wants of this army, and the efforts made to supply them. Our absentees are returning, and I hope the earnest and beautiful appeal made to the country in your proclamation may stir up the whole people, and that they may see their duty and perform it. Nothing is wanted but that their fortitude should equal their bravery to insure the success of our cause. We must expect reverses, even defeats. They are sent to teach us wisdom and prudence, to call forth greater energies, and to prevent our falling into greater disasters. Our people have only to be true and united, to bear manfully the misfortunes incident to war, and all will come right in the end. I know how prone we are to censure, and how ready to blame, others for the non-fulfillment of our expectations. This is unbecoming in a generous people, and I grieve to see its expression. The general remedy for the want of success in a military commander is his removal. This is natural, and in many instances proper; for no matter what may be the ability of the officer, if he loses the confidence of his troops disaster must sooner or later ensue.

I have been prompted by these reflections more than once since my return from Pennsylvania to propose to your Excellency the propriety of selecting another commander for this army. I have seen and heard of expressions of discontent in the public journals at the result of the expedition. I do not know how far this feeling extends to the Army. My brother officers have been too kind to report it, and so far the troops have been too generous to exhibit it. It is fair, however, to suppose that it does exist, and success is so necessary to us that nothing should be left undone to secure it. I, therefore, in all sincerity, request your Excellency to take measures to supply my place. I do this with the more earnestness, because no one is more aware than myself of my inability to discharge the duties of my position. I cannot even accomplish what I myself desire. How can I fulfill the expectations of others? In addition, I sensibly feel the growing failure of my bodily strength. I have not yet recovered from the attack I experienced the past spring. I am becoming more and more incapable of exertion, and am thus prevented from making the personal examination, and giving the personal supervision to the operations in the field which I feel to be necessary. I am so dull, that in undertaking to use the eyes of others I am frequently misled.

Everything, therefore, points to the advantage to be derived from a new commander, and I the more anxiously urge the matter upon your Excellency from my belief that a younger and abler man than myself can readily be obtained. I know that he will have as gallant and brave an army as ever existed to second his efforts, and it would be the happiest day of my life to see at its head a worthy leader—one that would accomplish more than I can perform and all that I have wished. I hope your Excellency will attribute my request to the true reason—the desire to serve my country and to do all in my power to insure the success of her righteous cause.

I have no complaints to make of any one but myself. I have received nothing but kindness from those above me, and the most considerate attention from my comrades and companions in arms. To your Excellency I am specially indebted for uniform kindness and consideration. You have done everything in your power to aid me in the work committed to my charge without omitting anything to promote the general welfare. I pray that your efforts may at length be crowned with success, and that you may long live to enjoy the thanks of a grateful people. With sentiments of great esteem, I am,

Very respectfully and truly, yours,
R. E. Lee

See below Davis's reply of August 11, 1863.

Source: [JD]

~

REFUSAL OF RESIGNATION: *"To ask me to substitute you by someone…
more fit to command… is to demand an impossibility"*

Confederate President Jefferson Davis
Richmond, Virginia
August 11, 1863

To General Robert E. Lee,
Commanding Army of Northern Virginia:

Yours of the 8th instant has just been received. I am glad that you concur so entirely with me as to the wants of our country in this trying hour, and am happy to add that after the first depression consequent upon our disasters in the West indications have appeared that our people will exhibit that fortitude which we agree in believing is alone needful to secure ultimate success.

It well became Sidney Johnston, when overwhelmed by a senseless clamor, to admit the rule that success is the test of merit; and yet there has been nothing which I have found to require a greater effort of patience than to bear the criticisms of the ignorant, who pronounce everything a failure which does not equal their expectations or desires, and can see no good result which is not in the line of their own imaginings. I admit the propriety of your conclusions that an officer who loses the confidence of his troops should have his position changed, whatever may be his ability; but when I read the sentence I was not at all prepared for the application you were about to make. Expressions of discontent in the public journals furnish but little evidence of the sentiment of the army. I wish it were otherwise, even though all the abuse of myself should be accepted as the results of honest observation.

Were you capable of stooping to it, you could easily surround yourself with those who would fill the press with your laudations, and seek to exalt you for what you had not done, rather than detract from the achievements which will make you and your army the subject of history and object of the world's admiration for generations to come.

I am truly sorry to know that you still feel the effects of the illness you suffered last spring, and can readily understand the embarrassments you experience in using the eyes of others, having been so much accustomed to make your own reconnoissances. Practice will, however, do much to relieve that embarrassment, and the minute knowledge of the country which you had acquired will render you less dependent for topographical information.

But suppose, my dear friend, that I were to admit, with all their implications, the points which you present, where am I to find that new commander who is to possess the greater ability which you believe to be required? I do not doubt the readiness with which you would give way to one who could accomplish all that you have wished, and you will do me the justice to believe that if Providence should kindly offer such a person for our use I would not hesitate to avail myself of his services.

My sight is not sufficiently penetrating to discover such hidden merit, if it exists, and I have but used to you the language of sober earnestness, when I have impressed upon you the propriety of avoiding all unnecessary exposure to danger, because I felt our country could not bear to lose you. To ask me to substitute you by someone in my judgment more fit to command, or who would possess more of the confidence of the army, or of the reflecting men of the country, is to demand an impossibility.

It only remains for me to hope that you will take all possible care of yourself, that your health and strength may be entirely restored, and that the Lord will preserve you for the important duties devolved upon you in the struggle of our suffering country for the independence of which we have engaged in war to maintain.

As ever, very respectfully and truly,

JEFF'N DAVIS

Source: [JD]

∽

NEW YEAR'S EVE: *"You ask 'how cannonading sounds?'"*

George M. Doff, U.S.A.
First Pennsylvania Artillery, Battery B
Near Culpepper, Virginia
December 31, 1863

[To _____]

Time passes very slowly here in camp. Nothing to excite or keep the mind enlivened. Far from home and friends, separated from all we hold dear on earth, what is it that binds us here? Why do we

After Canned Goods

156

find so many volunteering to leave their homes, wives, children, parents, and sweethearts, to camp on the field of battle, to face the cannon's mouth, to undergo hunger, thirst, and every deprivation, and perhaps death in its worst form? Can anyone imagine it is the choice of these men to live such a life? I answer, it is not in human nature: there must be something else to lead them on. Is it love of their country? I think it is. When true men see an armed force rising up to destroy that government under which they live, and for which their forefathers fought, they cannot stand still and see their country go to ruin without a struggle: none but cowards or traitors would do it. We have had a hard struggle, but the times are brightening. We look forward and dream of peace! May it come with all its blessings!

You ask "how cannonading sounds?" You must fancy you hear a hundred thunders at once, and as many hissing serpents flying through the air; then as many little thunders all around you, for the bursting of shells, to say nothing of the fire of the musketry and disaster surrounding you; and then you have but & faint idea of it!

Source: [SL]

~

A Dead Shot.

1864

RETURNING FROM GENERAL SHERMAN'S RAID: *"I, a slaveholder, when the war began, found and freed a negro one day during our 'raid'"*

Will. M. McLain, U.S.A.
32nd Ohio Volunteers Infantry
February 1864

[To _____]

Do you suppose that it was without a thought of the hated race of "Abolitionists" that I, a slaveholder, when the war began, found and freed a negro one day during our "raid" through Miss.? He was handcuffed and tied to a tree on the bank of Chunkalo Creek, where his master had left him: when our cavalry came up he was trying to "run him off to Georgy."

I went with him a mile or so to find a key to unlock his handcuffs, and brought them in as a relic for a very kind friend of mine, Mrs. Ex-governor Harvey, of Wisconsin, who is staying here devoting her time and money to alleviating the hardships of the soldiers. God bless her!

Next, I found myself put in charge of *seven thousand refugee negroes!* with two hundred and fifty teams, of every description under the sun, and found it devolve on me to get these "grown-up children"

158

from their camps in the morning into column, on the road, and then in the evening to get them into camp again, for five long days: until at last I thought them safely within sight of the frowning battlements of Vicksburg, and turned them over to Colonel Thomas, chief of contrabands in these parts. I never worked so hard in all my life, as I did those five days, and never expect to again.

I don't say it was exactly a "labor of love"; but I found that I could understand and handle them better than more Northern-bred men; and so I conceived it my duty to tell the colonel so, and he immediately set me at it. I could fill sheets with an account of those five days, but am filling too many already, and must postpone rendering an account of my command until some other time.

But I have been "superseded": indeed I was on the day I reached Vicksburg, by one of the best and noblest women I ever knew, Mrs. Ex-governor Harvey, of Wisconsin. She has spent time and fortune, freely, for the last two years or more, in behalf of soldiers; and incidentally of refugees, either black or white. She, with Colonels Thomas and Ridgely, took charge of the latter, and separated or rather scattered them over the plantations near Vicksburg. There they now are at work.

Source: [SL]

⌇

READING CAMP: *"Altogether we have received the name of the literary squad"*

Charles Berry Senior, U.S.A.
Seventh Iowa Infantry
Prospect, Tennessee
April 14, 1864

Dear Father,

I received your letter last night which is the second one that I have had from you since I left. If I had one each day I should not get tired of opening them & reading them if they are from Iowa they are very welcome visitors but like angels visits few & far between. I wrote a letter to you yesterday but after I received this I thought that I must write again. I have wrote quite a number to different persons in the country but have received no answers. We get mail here every day; it is then taken to headquarters & each company's mail given to that company's orderly & then distributed by him....

You said something about Leonard Parker having sold out did he ever say anything to you about some money that he owed to me for rail making? I made him 1,880 rails & he only paid me for 1,500 when he counted them. There was a deep snow & he did not find them all & he promised if he found the rest he would hand the balance of the money to you. I know that the rails are there & he should have paid to you 3 dollars & 80 cents; perhaps he has but the next time you write let me know I have got with a good mess of boys, 8 of us; they are not a swearing blackguarding set at all with Stewart excepted. They are quite the reverse, more inclined to study & improve their mental faculties. We have had several debating schools in our shanty since we came here & we study grammar some & arithmetic.

One of our mess sent to Fowler & Wells & got a couple of Phonographic Books & we are just beginning to see a dawn of sense in that branch. We have had them only 4 or 5 days & were entirely ignorant of it, all of us, so we are not advanced in reading or writing it yet. Altogether we have received the name of the literary squad which sounds blackguarding.

Shanty just below us...is known by the name of Gambling Saloon. I have just been down to the guard house & saw one from the aforesaid place with his arms tied & fastened in a standing position & I thought that I would sooner be studying grammar or Phonography by which they try to ridicule us than to be in his place for running the picket lines or some other misdemeanor. I am perfectly well & hope that this may find you all the same.

Source: [ETC] http://etext.lib.virginia.edu/etcbin/toccer-new2?id =Se64d14.sgm&images=images/modeng&data=/texts/english/ modeng/parsed&tag=public&part=1&division=div1

Charles Berry Senior, U.S.A.
Seventh Iowa Infantry
Near Reseca, Georgia
May 17, 1864

Dear Father—

I take another opportunity of writing to you. The chances that we have of sending letters is very limited. The mails leave here now just when it happens. I am still in the enjoyment of good health & strength & hope that all of you at home can say the same. Perhaps you have received the last letter I wrote; if so you will see that we were then expecting some hard fighting. Some of it we have had. I have not seen a part of what is called the horrors of war. Luckily I have not been called upon to suffer myself but alas how many of our brave boys have. I still have but very narrowly escaped almost miraculously been spared my life. I have heard the hissing of bullets the shrieking of shells & the loud bellowing of artillery.

I think that the fighting has for some time subsided. The rebels as far as we know have retreated all except a rear guard of them which they have left to harass us & prevent us from rapidly pursuing them. I heard our Lieutenant say that it was believed that their main army has left for Richmond but it is not surely known. For 8 days there has been more or less fighting. Our regiment has been principally here at Calhoun Ferry; the heaviest fighting has been at Resaca. Last Saturday our regiment was put to support a battery that was planted to shell the rebels out of their fort down here & we were very much exposed to the replies of rebel shell. Five of our regiment killed & 3 wounded with a shell. One of the killed had both of his legs ripped from his body. We were ordered to lay flat down face to the ground & while we were in that position a whole or large piece of shell struck the ground about four feet from my head in a direct line, plowed a ditch in the ground on the top for 6 feet. Then only four feet from us it ricocheted & just marvelously glanced over our heads all done of course with the quickness of lightning. The only harm that it did it almost drove the dirt into the pores of our skin making a sharp burning sensation. If it had not glanced it must unavoidably have struck my head or shoulder.

On Sunday morning we crossed the river on pontoon bridges & found the rebels close on the other side. Our Company was sent out skirmishing & only one man wounded while we were out. The rest of the regiment were engaged & lost 54 killed & wounded. They drove the rebels however & killed & wounded full as many of them. We were skirmishing by the flank & when the battle was going on we were nearly in rear of the rebels. The brush was so thick where we was that we could not see far ahead & we got too far round to the right. It is a wonder that when the rebels retreated they did not happen to come upon us & take us all prisoners; there was nothing in the world to prevent them. If they had known where we were only one company of us we could have offered but very little resistance. We were so much in the rear of them that the bullets of our men came over the rebels & whistled around us. We came out of the wood to an opening & the rebels had retreated.

Then came the scene of the killed & wounded. I can not describe it so I will not attempt but if it may be called satisfaction I saw many of the rebels in their death agonies. One poor fellow begged of us to kill him. He said he would rather be dead than laying there. Though they had been fighting against us I thought

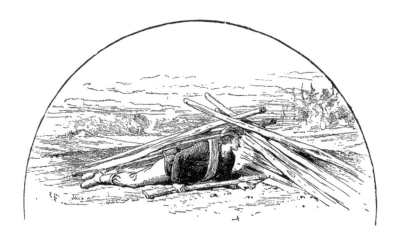

it was enough to soften the heart of the hardest man to see even a rebel in such a condition.

Paper is very scarce I must stop. I could fill one volume nearly. I shall not be able to write home regular but you have the chance of writing regular to me & I wish you to do it.

Source: [ETC]

⟿

BATTLE OF MILLIKEN'S BEND: *"We are in much more danger than white troops"*

Lieutenant Dengal McCall, U.S.A.
66th U.S. Colored Regiment
Milliken's Bend, Louisiana
April 19, 1864

[To _____]

Another twilight and moonlight has gone, and my letter is not finished. Last night I stopped writing to assist in putting up earthworks. We are only about 300 strong, and 1,500 are reported as marching against us. Possibly, ere this leaves my tent, we will have suffered the fate of the troops at Fort Pillow. It is currently reported that the fort was taken by the rebels, and the garrison massacred. If I must lose my life thus, I will not die begging; and if this report be true, I look for the time when they will be rewarded. There seems to be excitement in camp. The adjutant is giving orders as to the disposition of the forces. I have my letter nearly done, and am ready for battle. We are in much more danger than white troops, because few of us together.

At Fort Pillow, Tennessee, on April 12, 1864, Confederate General Nathan Bedford Forrest's troops overwhelmed the Union forces there and then massacred black soldiers who had surrendered. (By the war's end, there were an estimated 180,000 African-American soldiers in the Union Army.)

Source: [SL]

~

WILDERNESS CAMPAIGN: *"The particulars of your plans I neither know or seek to know"*

President Abraham Lincoln
Washington, D.C.
April 30, 1864

To Lieutenant General Ulysses S. Grant

Not expecting to see you again before the Spring campaign opens, I wish to express in this way, my entire satisfaction with what you have done up to this time, so far as I understand it. The particulars of your plans I neither know or seek to know. You are vigilant and self-reliant; and, pleased with this, I wish not to obtrude any constraints or restraints upon you. While I am very anxious that any great disaster, or the capture of our men in great numbers, shall be avoided, I know these points are less likely to escape your attention than they would be mine—If there is anything wanting which is within my power to give, do not fail to let me know it.

And now with a brave army, and a just cause, may God sustain you.

Yours very truly,
A. LINCOLN

Source: [AL]

~

THE DEATH OF J. E. B. STUART: *"to me in particular, his loss is irreparable"*

Phillip H. Powers, C.S.A.
Quartermaster, Cavalry Corps
Sunday, May 15, 1864

My Dear Wife—

The Sabbath moon opens upon us sadly this morning, and with a heart depressed with a dark and bitter grief I long to commune with some heart which can sympathize with me—We heard yesterday of the death of our noble leader, Genl. Stuart. And the sad news has thrown a gloom upon us all. Since the death of the lamented Jackson, no event, no disaster has so affected me. Jackson was a great loss to his country and the cause. Genl. Stuart is a great loss to his country—but to us, who have been intimately associated with him—to me in particular, his loss is irreparable for in him, I have lost my best friend in the army. I cannot realize that he is gone, that I am to see his gallant figure or hear his cheering voice no more—"God's will be done." A great man has fallen, and his faults are now swallowed up and forgotten in the recollection of his eminent virtues—his glorious valor and patriotism. May God in His mercy comfort his poor widow! My heart sorrows for her as for one very near to me.

The corps organization of the Cavalry is suspended for the present. The personal staff being assigned temporarily to the different Cavalry division. Our Quarter Master Department as it is for the present.

The two armies here still confront each other in line of battle though there has been no serious engagements since Thursday when Genl. Johnson's division was repelled and himself and many of his men captured the position and some of the artillery was recovered but not the provisions. Though in the same day we repulsed every other attack.

It has been raining for three days and you can hardly imagine how uncomfortable lying in the mud and wet every day. Fortunately my neuralgia attack has been worn itself out and affects me but very slightly though I am worn out and wearied in mind…Oh if it could all end…[The soldiers] have been in lines of battle exposed to all the inclemency of the weather, first the insufferable heat and now the drenching rains. And yet they stand and fight. And the wounded and the maimed and the dying lie around on that cold wet ground. No one to minister to their wounds and the last breath is caught by the passing and no listening ear of affection the sound. How long will a merciful God persist this war?…

Imboden has repulsed the enemy in the Valley and driven them to the Potomac. All other army news you can learn from the papers much better than I can. I saw Brother James yesterday….I have written you repeatedly our moves, but fear the letters will hardly reach you. I read yours of the 6th….And I am rejoiced that during all this turmoil and excitement in Richmond, you are in a place so far removed from this scene of danger. And hope you are getting along comfortably. Love to the children and kisses for the babes….

God be with you, my good wife.

Ever Yours

Source: [VS] http://valley.lib.virginia.edu/papers/A0326 {Copyright 1999 by the Rector and Visitors of the University of Virginia}

THE BATTLE OF THE WILDERNESS: *"I did not know how much I loved you"*

Lieutenant Charles De Mott, U.S.A.
First New York Artillery
May 1864

To His Wife

How grateful I feel this morning, no tongue can tell. I cannot give you a detailed account of the great battle going on for the last eight days—the battles of the Wilderness.

Fighting is still going on at the front, and we are expecting every moment to go in again. We have been for eight days on the front line of battle: last night we were relieved; unharnessed our horses, and gave our men an opportunity to sleep. For *four* days we have been in position, and fought where we could not raise our heads above our works without being shot at. Many a rebel bullet has whistled past my head so near, I could almost feel the wind of it! I have no time to tell of narrow escapes; "suffice it to say," *you yet have a husband* and our little boy a father, with an unshattered mind and body.

I have received compliments from officers of high rank: I tell you this not to boast, for *I feel humble,* but that you may feel proud. We captured, yesterday, 7,000 prisoners and thirty pieces of artillery.

Thoughts of my family come to my mind while in the midst of battle, nerving me to nobly dare the dangers that surround me. I did not know how much I loved you; you must have then been praying for me. I felt the affections of my heart welling up as pure and warm as ever. Dangers are not yet past. Continue to plead with my Heavenly Father for my welfare. I have great hopes of returning safely to the bosom of my family; but if I never do, I know I shall not be forgotten away down in the vista of the future; when my body has mingled for years with the dust of the brave men who have fallen in battle, you will think of me.

News has just come in from the front; the enemy has fallen back. Now for Richmond!

YOUR AFFECTIONATE HUSBAND

De Mott was killed June 3, 1864.

Source: [SL]

Lieutenant Anson Tyler Hemingway, U.S.A.
70th U.S. Colored Regiment
Vidalia, Louisiana
May 17, 1864

[To ____]

There has been a party of guerrillas prowling about here, stealing horses and mules from the leased plantations.
A scouting party was sent out from here, in which was a company of colored cavalry, commanded by the colonel of a colored regiment. After marching some distance, they came upon the party of whom they were in pursuit. There were seventeen prisoners captured and shot by the colored soldiers. When the guerrillas were first seen, the colonel told them in a loud tone of voice to "Remember Fort Pillow." And they did: all honor to them for it.

If the Confederacy wish to fight us on these terms, we are glad to know it, and will try and do our part in the contest. I do not admire the mode of warfare, but know of no other way for us to end the war than to retaliate.

Hemingway (1844–1926) took part in the battle for Vicksburg in 1863. (See the note on the Fort Pillow massacre in reference to Dengal McCall's letter of April 19, 1864, above.)

Source: [SL]

∿

COLD HARBOR: *"The enemy, I think, outfight us, but we outnumber them"*

Captain Charles Francis Adams, Jr., U.S.A.
Headquarters, Army of Potomac
Hanover Town, Virginia
May 29, 1864

To His Father, Charles Francis Adams, Sr.

The campaign to us here gradually unfolds itself. Grant and Meade discuss and decide, but keep their own counsel, and no one knows whether tomorrow the Army is to fight, to march, or to rest. Meanwhile marching now seems to be the order of the day, and since day before yesterday Head Quarters have moved thirty odd miles, turning all the exterior lines of Richmond and bringing us down to the interior line of the Chickahominy. Here we rest for today. Up to this time General Grant seems to have looked on this campaign in Virginia as one necessarily to be made up of the hardest kind of fighting, combined with all the generalship which he could command, and, as we were numerically the strongest, we might as well do the fighting first as last, pounding and maneuvering at the same time. If this was his idea, I think the wisdom of it is becoming apparent. I cannot believe that his operations have been or now are conducted on any fixed plan. He seems to have one end in view—the capture of Richmond and the destruction of Lee's army; but I imagine his means to that end undergo daily changes and no man in this Army, but Meade perhaps, is even able to give grounds for a guess as to whether we are to approach Richmond from this side or from the other.

Meanwhile, though Grant expected hard fighting, I have no idea that he expected anything like the fighting and the slaughter which took place in the Wilderness and at Spottsylvania. He had never seen anything like it in the West, and the fierce, stubborn resistance we met far surpassed his expectation. Meade knew better what he had to expect and in fighting for him those battles were, I imagine, of incalculable assistance to Grant. Today, as near as I can see, results stand as follows: these two great armies

have pounded each other nearly to pieces for many days; neither
has achieved any real success over the other on the field of battle.
Our loss has probably been greater than theirs, for ours has been
the offensive; but we have a decided balance of prisoners and
captured artillery in our favor. The enemy, I think, outfight us, but
we outnumber them, and, finally, within the last three days one
witnesses in this Army as it moves along all the results of a victory,
when in fact it has done only barren fighting. For it has done the
one thing needful before the enemy—it has advanced. The result
is wonderful. Hammered and pounded as this Army has been;
worked, marched, fought and reduced as it is, it is in better spirits
and better fighting trim today than it was in the first day's fight in
the Wilderness.

Strange as it seems to me, it is, I believe, yet the fact, that this
Army is now just on its second wind, and is more formidable than
it ever was before. This I see on every march and I attribute it to
movement in advance after heavy, though barren, fighting.

With the enemy it is otherwise. Heavier fighting, harder
marching, and greater privations—for with them deficiency in
numbers was only to be made good by redoubled activity—two
men with them have done the work of three with us—all these
have led only to movements to the rear, to the abandonment of line

GETTING READY FOR SUPPER.

after line until now they find themselves with their backs against Richmond. Naturally this discourages troops, particularly coming after as hard fighting as they know how to do, and as a result we now get, as I am informed, from all sources but one story, and that of discouragement and exhaustion. The enemy is getting off his fight. What is to come next? Will Lee try to revive the spirits of his men and the fortunes of his Army by taking the offensive? Will he try to repeat the story of the Chickahominy and the six days' fighting? What does Grant mean next to do?

I have always noticed that when I try to divine the future of military operations I am invariably wrong, and so I long ago gave up trying. Of a few things though I feel pretty sure. Stonewall Jackson is dead, Grant is not McClellan, nor is Meade McDowell. Grant will not let his Army be idle, nor will he allow the initiative to be easily taken out of his hands, and if he can outfight Meade, he will do more than he was ever able to do yet when his troops were more numerous, in better heart and much fresher than they now are. Accordingly we find ourselves approaching the climax of the campaign, under circumstances which certainly seem to me hopeful. The next few days will probably develop Grant's final move, the line on which he means to approach Richmond and the point at which he means, unless Lee out-generals him, to have the final fight. I don't believe he will allow time to slip away or Lee to repair damages. I do believe that while the Army is resting today, it is drawing breath for the great struggle and on the eve of great movements and decisive results.

Things meanwhile work in the Army charmingly. Grant is certainly a very extraordinary man. He does not look it and might pass well enough for a dumpy and slouchy little subaltern, very fond of smoking. Neither do I know that he shows it in his conversation, for he never spoke to me and doesn't seem to be a very talkative man anyhow. They say his mouth shows character. It may, but it is so covered with beard that no one can vouch for it. The truth is, he is in appearance a very ordinary looking man, one who would attract attention neither in the one way or the other. Not knowing who it is, you would not pronounce him insignificant, and knowing who it is, it would require some study to find in his appearance material for hero worship, though there is about his face no indication of weakness or lack of force. He has not nearly so strong a head and face as Humphreys', for instance, who at once strikes you as a man of force. In figure Grant is comical. He sits a horse well, but in walking he leans forward and toddles. Such being his appearance, however, I do not think that any intelligent person could watch him, even from such a distance as mine, without concluding that he is a remarkable man. He handles those around him so quietly and well, he so evidently has the faculty of disposing of work and managing men, he is cool and quiet, almost stolid and as if stupid, in danger, and in a crisis he is one against whom all around, whether few in number or a great army as here, would instinctively lean. He is a man of the most exquisite judgment and tact. See how he has handled this Army. He took command under the most unfavorable circumstances—jealousy between East and West; the Army of the Potomac and the Army of the Southwest; that general feeling that the officers from the West were going to swagger over those here and finally that universal envy which success creates and which is always ready to carp at it.

The moment I came to Head Quarters I saw that, though nothing was said, yet the materials were all ready for an explosion at the first mistake Grant made. All this has passed away and now Grant has this army as firmly as ever he had that of the Southwest. He has effected this simply by the exercise of tact and good taste. He has humored us, he has given some promotions, he has made no parade of his authority, he has given no orders except through Meade, and Meade he treats with the utmost confidence and deference. The result is that even from the most jealously disposed and most indiscreet of Meade's staff, not a word is heard against Grant. The result is of inestimable importance. The army has a head and confidence in that head. It has leaders and there is no discord among those leaders. We seem to have gotten rid of jealousy and all now seem disposed to go in with a will to win....

Source: [CAL-2]

~

Captain Charles Francis Adams, Jr., U.S.A.
Headquarters, Army of Potomac
Cold Harbor, Virginia
June 4, 1864

To His Father, Charles Francis Adams, Sr.

Since my last of a week ago I have heard nothing and received nothing from you. Your letters evidently go astray, but where to does not yet appear. Mine was written from near Hanover Town; since then Head Quarters have twice moved, and we now find ourselves the same distance from Richmond, but more to the left and near the scene of McClellan's disaster at Gaines's Mills. We are again edging along a system of earthworks to the left, the two armies moving by the flank in parallel lines of battle. This whole country round here presents a most extraordinary spectacle in the matter of entrenchments. You doubtless hear a great deal about rifle pits. These scar the whole country all along the road of these two armies. You see them confronting each other in long lines on every defensible position and you never seem to get through them. A rifle pit, in fact, is in the perfection to which they are now carried in these armies, nothing more nor less than most formidable fortifications, alive with infantry and bristling with artillery. The instant our infantry, for instance, get into position, they go to work with axes and spades and in a very short time there springs up in front of them a wooden barricade, made out of fence rails, felled trees or any material in reach of men who know what danger is and feel it near them; and in rear and front of this a trench is dug, the dirt from the rear being thrown over to the front, so as to bank it up and make it impenetrable to musketry and, except at the top, to artillery. This cover is anywhere from four to six feet high, is often very neatly made, and is regularly bastioned out, as it were, for artillery. As fast as a position is won, it is fortified in this way. For defense the same thing is done.

The other day I rode down to the front and passed four lines of these entrenchments, all deserted and useless, before I came to the fifth, where the line of battle then was, which had just been taken from the enemy, and which they were already confronting by a new one. In this country, however, even these pits in the hands of an enemy are rarely seen. This is, as a country, the meanest of the mean—sandy and full of pine barrens, exhausted by man and not attractive by nature, it is sparsely peopled, broken, badly watered, heavily wooded with wretched timber, and wholly uninteresting. In it you can see no enemy, for he is covered by a continual forest. He may be in front in any force, or in almost any kind of works or position, but you cannot see him. There is and can be almost no open fighting here, the party acting on the defensive having always the enormous advantage of cover, which he is not likely to forego.

We crossed the Pamunkey a week ago today and the Army has since been living and fighting in this wretched region. The weather has been very hot and dry, and the dust has accordingly been intense. The men have suffered much in marching and the incessant fatigue and anxiety of the campaign, combined with the unhealthy food, must soon begin to tell on the health of the Army. Meanwhile the fighting has been incessant, the question simply being one of severity. Yesterday we made a general attack and suffered a severe repulse. Today little seems to be going on. The Army all this time seems to be improving in morale. I do not see at any rate so much straggling as I did at Spotsylvania. To be sure the stock of the country seems to suffer badly, and I see more dead pelts than I do live sheep, more feathers by the roads than fowls in the yards; but I no longer see the throngs of stragglers which then used to frighten me. The country however is terribly devastated. This Army is, I presume, no worse than others, but it certainly leaves no friends behind it. I fear that the inhabitants are stripped of everything except that which can neither be stolen or destroyed. This is the work of the stragglers, the shirks and the cowards, the bullies and ruffians of the Army.

As I now move with Head Quarters all my marching is very different from any I ever did before. Grant and Meade usually ride together, and as they ride too fast for me, I send a party to keep along with them and then come up at my leisure. So they push ahead surrounded by a swarm of orderlies and in a cloud of dust, pushing through columns and trains, and I follow as fast as I can. In this way I am forced to see all there is to see of this Army, laboring by long trains of wagons and artillery and interminable columns of infantry, now winding along through the woods by the roadside and now taking to the fields; waiting half an hour for a sufficient break in a column to enable one to cross the road, and at all times wondering over the perfect flood of humanity which flows by me by the hour in the form of a great Army. It is very wearing and tiresome, this always moving in a procession. One gets hot and peevish. Human patience cannot endure such wear and tear. One is greatly impressed at these times with the "pride, pomp and circumstance of glorious war." There is abundance of material to be seen, men and muskets, horses and artillery; but for "pride and pomp," that is lacking enough! The men look dirty and tired; they toil along in loose, swaying columns and are chiefly remarkable for a most wonderful collection of old felt hats in every stage of dilapidation. Their clothes are torn, dusty and shabby; few

Well Fixed

carry knapsacks and most confine their luggage to a shelter-tent and blanket which is tied in a coil over one shoulder. There is in the sight of such a column marching much that is picturesque and striking; but such features do not at first appear and never in the shape in which one imagines them.

Grant and Meade usually start about seven o'clock and get into camp at about two. They stop at houses on the road and wait for reports or to consult. I pass much of my time noticing Grant during these halts. For the last few days he has evidently been thinking very hard. I never noticed this before. Formerly he always had a disengaged expression in his face; lately he has had an intent, abstracted look, and as he and Meade sit round on our march I see Grant stroking his beard, puffing at his cigar and whittling at small sticks, but with so abstracted an air that I see well that they are with him merely aids to reflection. In fact as he gets down near Richmond and approaches the solution of his problem, he has need to keep up a devil of a thinking.

Yesterday he attacked the enemy and was decidedly repulsed. He always is repulsed when he attacks their works, and so are they when they attack his. The course of the campaign seems to me to have settled pretty decisively that neither of these two armies can, in the field, the one acting defensively and the other offensively, gain any great advantage. Fighting being equal, it becomes therefore a question of generalship.

To capture Richmond Grant must do with Lee what he did with Pemberton, he must outgeneral him and force him to fight him on his own ground. This all of us uninformed think he could accomplish by crossing the James and taking Richmond in the rear, and accordingly we are most eager that that should be done. Grant seems to hesitate to do this and to desire to approach by this side. His reasons of course we do not know, but they yesterday cost this army six thousand men. Feeling that we cannot beat the rebels by hard, point-blank pounding before Richmond, we are most anxious to find ourselves in some position in which they must come out and pound us or give way. The south bank of the James seems to hold out to us hopes of supplies, rest and success, and we are anxiously watching for movements pointing in that direction. While Butler holds Bermuda Hundreds I shall hope that he does so to keep there a foothold for us, and shall continue to hope for another flank move to the left every day. When it comes I shall look for the crisis of the campaign.

Meanwhile I see nothing to shake my faith in Grant's ultimate capture of Richmond, and even this delay and yesterday's false step seem rather like some of the man's proceedings in the Southwest, when he went on the apparent principle of trying everything, but leaving nothing untried. At present there is one thing to be said of this campaign and its probable future. In it the rebellion will feel the entire strength of the Government exerted to the utmost. If Grant takes Richmond, even without a battle, I think Lee's army will be essentially destroyed; for they will lose their prestige. The defense of Richmond keeps them alive. They will never again fight as they now do, when once that is lost.

Thus to me the campaign seems now to be narrowed down to a question of the capture of Richmond and that to a question of generalship. As to endurance and fighting qualities, the two armies are about equal, all things being considered, and the enemy's lack of numbers is compensated for by the fact of their acting on the defensive....

Source: [CAL-2]

～

ATLANTA CAMPAIGN: *"if I was home again I could help you in so many ways that I never thought of before"*

Chauncey H. Cooke, U.S.A.
25th Infantry, Wisconsin
Pine Woods of Georgia
June 6, 1864

Dear Parents—

I am off duty and have had six hours of refreshing nap. Henry Morse has just been to see me and asked me to say nothing that will get to his folks about his health. He is bad off with bowel trouble but he doesn't want his people to know of it. They have cut

our rations in half and every fellow is hungry. Every few days our cavalry raiders capture a lot of smoked meat and corn pones and lots of the boys overeat because it's good and they are down sick. Henry is one of them. The trouble is we can't eat here like we can in Wisconsin. If we eat a good fill we are off our feed for a day or two. When our rations are short the boys go to the quartermaster's and if they have a dime fill up on pie and cake and it's regular poison to them.

I dreamed last night about the cheese which you wrote about in the letter I got three days ago. Sure I would like a taste of it but, Mother, I wish you would stop making cheese with all your other work. It's too much, Mother. I don't remember that I helped you very much in such work but it seems to me if I was home again I could help you in so many ways that I never thought of before and I will be home again some day. I am sure we soldiers will have good times again to pay for this. This war will not last always. Gen. Grant is flaxing them in Virginia, and I saw the other day in an Atlanta paper that Gen. Sherman could "outflank Hell," so there is a show that we will outflank Hood and get into Atlanta before long. Let not the people of the North find fault and wonder why we don't press on faster. Great Heavens, think what we have to do. I used to wonder why the Potomac army did not move faster. Then I knew nothing of marching in armies of one or two hundred thousand men. Let people stop and think about these things, then they will be more patient.

Let me tell you something about it. Sherman has five army corps of from 15 to 25 thousand men in each corps. Each corps is following in the same direction on parallel roads from 3 to 5 miles apart. Each corps means a string of men, four abreast, of from eight to ten miles long. There is an army of rebels posted on every one of these roads with cannon at every crossroad, cavalry dashing in upon our flanks and sharpshooters picking our men off at every opening where the pine forest comes within a half or quarter of a mile of the road. You can see the time we are having. If one of the corps is stopped by trees fallen across the road so the cannon or the cavalry cannot pass, couriers are sent to stop all the other corps until the way is cleared. All the bridges are burned by the retreating rebels and have to be rebuilt, which causes a delay. Sometimes we use pontoons, boats made of canvas anchored in the rivers with planks stretched from one to the other. Where the roads are obstructed they fall timber on both sides for miles and sharpen the limbs so we can't get thru. A dozen times every day we come to a halt, for what we don't know. It's a safe guess that it's a broken wagon axle, a crippled cannon or a played-out cassion truck. No questions are asked. We are only too glad to fall down on our faces and snatch a few minutes sleep. There are more delays from ammunition and "sow belly" wagons breaking down than from any other one cause. Then the guerrillas are forever attacking our rear guard, and sometimes bodies of men and batteries have to be sent back to help them out. All this means a delay.

Sister Dora wrote that father expected to buy a couple of cows of Mr. Harvey. I think it a good deal as I shall want a lot of milk, butter and cheese when I come home, if I do, this winter. Everybody thinks the rebellion on its last legs, and that means the end of it when we get into its strongest and last defense, Atlanta.

An orderly has just ridden up to the Brigade Headquarters and, as it may mean something serious, will close for this time. Please send stamps in your next.

Your son,
CHAUNCEY

Source: Soldierstudies.org [SS]

∼

GOD'S WILL: *"The purposes of the Almighty are perfect, and must prevail"*

President Abraham Lincoln
Executive Mansion
Washington, D. C.
September 4, 1864

To Eliza P. Gurney

My esteemed friend—

I have not forgotten—probably never shall forget—the very impressive occasion when yourself and friends visited me on a Sabbath forenoon two years ago. Nor has your kind letter, written nearly a year later, ever been forgotten. In all, it has been your purpose to strengthen my reliance on God. I am much indebted to the good Christian people of the country for their constant prayers and consolations; and to no one of them, more than to yourself. The purposes of the Almighty are perfect, and must prevail, though we erring mortals may fail to accurately perceive them in advance. We hoped for a happy termination of this terrible war long before this; but God knows best, and has ruled otherwise. We shall yet acknowledge His wisdom and our own error therein. Meanwhile we must work earnestly in the best light He gives us, trusting that so working still conduces to the great ends He ordains. Surely He intends some great good to follow this mighty convulsion, which no mortal could make, and no mortal could stay.

Your people—the Friends—have had, and are having, a very great trial. On principle, and faith, opposed to both war and oppression, they can only practically oppose oppression by war. In this hard dilemma, some have chosen one horn, and some the other. For those appealing to me on conscientious grounds, I have done, and shall do, the best I could and can, in my own conscience, under my oath to the law. That you believe this I doubt not; and believing it, I shall still receive, for our country and myself, your earnest prayers to our Father in heaven.

Your sincere friend
A. LINCOLN

Eliza Gurney (1801–1881) was a Quaker who visited Lincoln at the White House in the fall of 1862.

Source: [AL]

~

ATLANTA CAMPAIGN: *"Atlanta is no place for families or non-combatants"*

General William Tecumseh Sherman, U.S.A.
Headquarters, Military Division of the Mississippi
In the Field, Atlanta
September 7, 1864

To General John Bell Hood, Commanding Confederate Army:

General:

I have deemed it to the interest of the United States that the citizens now residing in Atlanta should remove, those who prefer it to go South, and the rest North. For the latter I can provide food and transportation to points of their election in Tennessee, Kentucky, or farther north. For the former I can provide transportation by cars as far as Rough and Ready, and also wagons; but that their removal may be made with as little discomfort as possible it will be necessary for you to help the families from Rough and Ready to the cars at Lovejoy's. If you consent I will undertake to remove all the families in Atlanta who prefer to go South to Rough and Ready, with all their movable effects, viz, clothing, trunks, reasonable furniture, bedding, &c., with their servants, white and black, with the proviso that no force shall be used toward the blacks one way or the other. If they want to go with their masters or mistresses they may do so, otherwise they will be sent away, unless they be men, when they may be employed by our quartermaster.

Atlanta is no place for families or non-combatants and I have no desire to send them North if you will assist in conveying them South. If this proposition meets your views I will consent to a truce in the neighborhood of Rough and Ready, stipulating that any wagons, horses, or animals, or persons sent there for the purposes herein stated shall in no manner be harmed or molested, you in your turn agreeing that any cars, wagons, or carriages, persons, or animals sent to the same point shall not be interfered with. Each of us might send a guard of, say, 100 men to maintain order, and limit the truce to, say, two days after a certain time appointed. I have authorized the mayor to choose two citizens to convey to you this letter and such documents as the mayor may forward in explanation, and shall await your reply.

> I have the honor to be, your obedient servant.
> *W. T. SHERMAN,*
> Major-General, Commanding

Source: [WOR]

~

Chauncey H. Cooke, U.S.A.
25th Infantry, Wisconsin
Marietta, Georgia
September 10, 1864

Dear Sister—

Your thrice welcome letter, so long looked for came last night, and the promised $2 came in it. I was really needing the money for little wants. When you offer these Georgians their money they smile sadly and shake their head. Now that Atlanta has fallen into our hands they feel that the South will be whipped and their money will be worthless.

Your letter had a lot of good news and I went over to read it to my foster mother, that is the woman who has given me so many good meals. She sat in a big armchair on the broad porch knitting some stockings. I sat down on the steps. When I looked up after reading the letter she was crying. She said, "You must have a good sister and how good it is that you boys from the North can get letters from home while our poor boys cannot write letters to their people at home nor receive any." She said, "I have not heard a word from my daughter who went to Atlanta with her sweetheart, nor from my husband for two months. I don't know if they are living or dead." I suppose there are a thousand women in this town who feel just as she does. There seem to be three or more in nearly every house.

I wrote father last week about the surrender of Atlanta. Since then we have had further particulars. The night before, our shells blew up two of their magazines and set fire to the big depot and burned a lot of their cars. For several days before the surrender and even now we can see clouds of smoke hanging over the city. Nearly the entire place is a burning ruin.

It is just two years today since our regiment was mustered into the service. One more year will let us out and less if the talk we hear of the Confederacy having its back broken proves true.

Day after tomorrow will be two months I am in this darned hospital. Expect to go to my regiment in a few days. A lot of the time here I have had the blues and still I am among the lucky ones to get away at all. On the hill the other side the railroad hundreds of poor fellows lie under little mounds newly made. They will never answer to bugle call any more and to them all troubles in this world are over.

Don't send any more money as we are soon to draw pay and I shall have a sum to send home. Everybody that can is is going to Atlanta to see the ruins.

The natives are in hopes of finding out something about their men who were in the rebel army. Some of the women are nearly crazy. Everybody rides in box cars or cattle cars. When the cars are full they climb on top.

My stomach is off today on account of eating some sour milk. I got it last night of a colored aunty on the picket line. This morning it was sour. I scalded it but it upset me.

A colored woman just came to the tent with my clothes she has been washing. She had a two-bushel basket full of clothes and carried it on her head. She was a yellow woman and the mother of six children. The three oldest, two girls and one boy, had been sold to a cotton planter in Alabama.

Washing Day in Camp.

One of the boys asked her if she cared and she replied, "Shua, honey, I loves my chilen just likes you mammy loves you." I am sure the poor woman's heart was full, for her eyes filled with tears. I thank God along with father and Elder Morse that Lincoln has made them free. She said her children was nearly as white as we, and that three of them had a white father. To think that these slaveholders buy and sell each other's bastard children is horrible. She took us by the hand and bid each of us goodbye and asked God to bless us and our mothers. I see and hear things every day that make me think of *Uncle Tom's Cabin*. Word has come that we are to be ready to go to Atlanta tomorrow or next day. The boys are making a great hurrah about it.

Direct to 25th Regiment, Wis. Vol., Atlanta, Ga. Goodbye, dear sister. And as the wretched slave mother said to me, I say to you, God bless you and all the rest.

Your brother,
CHAUNCEY

Source: Soldierstudies.org [SS]

～

THE PRESIDENTIAL ELECTION: *"offer terms with traitors in arms against the United States government! Oh! no, no, no!"*

Edwin Marsh, U.S.A.
Army of the Cumberland
West Virginia
September 15, 1864

To His Aunt Julia

I have been so busy making out the company pay-rolls, that I have not had time to write before. Well, are you aware that the time for election is drawing near, and the soldiers have received the news and the result of the Chicago Convention; and almost all with whom I have spoken on the subject, who *were* McClellan men before, are, since his acceptance of the peace platform, strong against him; for how can a soldier be a peace man when they are fighting to crush the rebellion by force of arms? Do you or anyone suppose I would be willing to give up all we have gained in this great struggle for liberty, Union, and the *dear* old flag? What! now lay down our arms and offer terms with traitors in arms against the United States government! Oh! no, no, no! The spirits of our murdered comrades would stand constantly before us, calling on us to avenge their death.

There was one little fellow killed in the battle of Winchester, as brave a little soldier as ever fired carbine; for *his sake* I will never vote for such men as McClellan and Pendleton.

There is no soldier or citizen more anxious for peace than I am, yet I want peace on such terms as we may dictate. Let the citizens of the North come out and carry the election at home, and the soldiers will do their part to elect Abraham Lincoln, the faithful ruler of the people. I am certain that if he be re-elected, the war will soon be ended. I will stake my life on it.

Aunt Julia, if it will not be giving you too much trouble, I should like you to ascertain the price of a really handsome cavalry sword; some of the *boys* are going to present our captain with one, and of course it should be a good one, for he is a soldier and a gentleman. To be a *soldier* and a *gentleman* is the only distinction of which I should be proud; indeed such honors I hope to claim. Is it not a title of which an American should be proud? I will close this epistle, and subscribe myself, along with Robert—two of the best *Union men* between Richmond and Canada—

YOUR AFFECTIONATE NEPHEW

Source: [SL]

Private Charles W. Baylor, C.S.A.
Camp Near New Market, Virginia
September 24, 1864

To His Friend Charles W. McGuffin

Dear Charlie—

I received yours of the 18th yesterday. I am sorry to tell you that your Brother John is no more. He was killed in the battle at Winchester, shot in the head I think, though I am not certain for I did not see him, though I was told by someone who professed to know, he lived but a very short time after he was struck.

I would have written to you immediately but I did not have time, I wrote home, and told my wife to tell Mary to write to you about and let you know the worst, I have but little good news to tell you, we had another hard fight on the 19th, were victorious until about three o'clock, the Yanks flanked us and we had to fall back which raised a perfect stampede. We captured wagons, ambulances, mules, horses, eighteen pieces of artillery & about 1,500 prisoners. Though fortune turned & we lost all the artillery that we captured & I believe as much more, lost ambulance, wagons, & I don't know what all…we got the prisoners out by hard work & had it not been that they were in front of the train we would of gotten more of it out of the way. We lost but very few prisoners & an unusual small number of killed & wounded. Though Company H lost—I think, its full share of in killed we took 11 men with myself into the fight. Out of that number there were two killed & one wounded. Sergeant B. F. Hupp & W. H. McClung were killed or I suppose McClung is dead by this time for he was shot in the head just above the right eye, the ball is in his head, he was insensible in fifteen minutes afterward that was about 9 o'clock in the morning, he was not dead at sundown but still insensible, & seemed to be dying, Jacob Runkle was wounded in the right shoulder slightly Colonel Williams was wounded in the right shoulder severely, Colonel Runk was left at Winchester supposed

to be mortally wounded in the side, Dr. Walls pronounced it mortal, Major Newton wounded in ankle, & it is feared that he will lose his foot.

I must close as it is getting late, I would like to give you a more detailed account of our doings in the Valley, but I have not got the time. I have not received a letter from home for almost a month have only got two letters from home since I left there.

We have only got one Major & one Colonel, Stuart Major 2nd Regiment Colonel Spungler of the 33rd Regiment.

I must Close, may God protect you is the humble prayer of

Your Friend

C. W. Baylor

∾

Private John P. Dull, C. S. A.
Fifth Virginia Infantry
Camp Near New Market
November 20, 1864

To His Wife

Dear Giney—

It is with pleasure that I take this opportunity to drop you a few lines to let you know how I am at this time thank the Lord I enjoy good health have been well ever since left home except a cold I have had right bad cold for some time other ways I have been hearty hoping this may find you all well. I hoped to have gotten a letter from you before now but have not I wrote you the ninth of this month Suppose you did not get it Since that time we have had a hard march down the valley we were near Winchester expected to have a fight but it turned out otherwise we are now in Camp where we was when I last wrote my feet became very sore on the march but are now well again, this is rainy wet weather here this is the Sabbath day things are quite still here today. And now Dear Giney I will tell you that I was quite surprised yesterday I walked out from Camp a few hundred yards about the middle of the day came back and what did I See why our old blue Box sitting on the wood pile this was very unexpected to me. But with a grateful heart I received it and now I return you my grateful thanks for your kindness it came in good time for I was hungry I invited Several of my Company to eat with me they said that the woman that made that Butter and Bread knew how to do it You have no idea how such things are appreciated in camp the men found that I had butter they would have take all I had in a short time if I would have let them You sent more butter than I thought I could use so I Spared one of the role. Sold two pound of it and loaned the rest out thought it would come good sometime. I let the men have it at 7 Dollars per pound it was selling at ten Dollars in camp but I thought it was too much for Soldiers to pay I found my overcoat alright I had written you not to send it for a while but suppose you did not get it in time since it is here I will keep it it is very good in camp but not on the march because it is heavy to carry. I looked in every pocket for a letter but could not find any Miller told me that there was some potatoes at Summerdeen for me but he had so much load he could not haul them, I am very glad to get as much as I did hoping to hear from you soon I will close my Prayer is that the Lord will bless you and take care of you all and save us all in heaven at last

as your ever affectionate
HUSBAND

[P.S.] I send Box by the wagon

Source: [VS] http://valley.lib.virginia.edu/papers/A6125

∽

CHRISTMAS PRESENT: *"the city of Savannah"*

Major General William T. Sherman, U.S.A.
Savannah, Georgia
December 22, 1864

To President Abraham Lincoln

I beg to present you, as a Christmas gift, the city of Savannah, with one hundred and fifty guns and plenty ammunition; and also about twenty-five thousand (25,000) bales of cotton.

W. T. SHERMAN,
Major-General

Source: [UR]

∽

President Abraham Lincoln
Executive Mansion
Washington, D. C.
December 26, 1864

To General William Tecumseh Sherman

My Dear General Sherman:—

Many, many thanks for your Christmas gift, the capture of Savannah.

When you were about leaving Atlanta for the Atlantic coast, I was anxious, if not fearful; but feeling that you were the better judge, and remembering that "nothing risked, nothing gained," I did not interfere. Now, the undertaking being a success, the honor is all yours; for I believe none of us went further than to acquiesce.

And taking the work of General Thomas into the count, as it should be taken, it is indeed a great success. Not only does it afford the obvious and immediate military advantages; but in showing to the world that your army could be divided, putting the stronger part to an important new service, and yet leaving enough to vanquish the old opposing force of the whole,—Hood's army,—it brings those who sat in darkness to see a great light. But what next?

I suppose it will be safe if I leave General Grant and yourself to decide.

Please make my grateful acknowledgments to your whole army of officers and men.

Yours very truly,
A. LINCOLN

Source: [AL]

~

1865

A PROMISE: *"all that was left of my friend lay before me on a stretcher in an ambulance"*

Lieutenant Oliver Willcox Norton, U.S.A.
Eighth United States Colored Troops
Chapin's Farm, Virginia
Sunday, January 15, 1865, midnight

To Elizabeth (Libby) Lane Norton

Dear Sister L.:—

My diary has ceased to be. It is now the middle of January, 1865, and I have made no entries in it since I left the hospital, and as I am about to send it to you lest it share the fate of my other diaries in the early part of the war, and in the hope that some of it may interest you, I can think of nothing better than to fill up a few more pages with some recollections, and records of the regiment, and of myself.

As you know from my letters, I reached the regiment on the 6th of October, having left the hospital before I was strong enough for duty in the line, with the expectation of being regimental adjutant. I found Lieutenant Evans already in the office, and while Major Wagner was deliberating whether it was best to return him to his company and make me adjutant, Lieutenant Burrows was made brigade quartermaster and the major at once detailed me to act as regimental quartermaster in his place, and "A. R. Q. M." I have been ever since.

The regiment was then lying in the works to the right of the rebel Fort Harrison, which was taken by our forces on the 29th of September, and the name since changed to Fort Burnham, in honor of Brigadier General Burnham, who was killed in the charge which captured the fort.

On the 13th of October the reconnoissance on the Darby Road was made. As a military success or a movement of importance in any respect, it is not worth mention, but it is a memorable day to me on account of the death of my dearest and best army friend. Captain A. G. Dickey.

The "Eighth" was deployed as skirmishers early in the morning and covered the front of the division. Three companies were held in reserve and Captain Dickey had command of those companies. I left my place at the train on learning that fighting was in progress and came up to the front to learn what was being done. I found the division in a belt of woods facing a line of the enemy's works and the skirmish line pushed well up to those works. The reserve was a few rods in rear of the line and they had remained in that position some three hours. The skirmishers were pretty well concealed and kept up a desultory fire wherever they could see any of the enemy, and the rebels did the same. An occasional bullet cut through the bushes near the reserves, but I did not think it a place of particular danger, or having no particular business I should not have been there. As it was I sat down on the ground by the captain and stayed two or three hours, and then thinking that not much more would be done that day and that I should have little enough time to get back to the train before night, I started to return. The captain said to me as I left, in that bantering style so common among soldiers, "Take care of yourself, Norton, this is no place for quartermasters," and I retorted in similar style. It was the last word he ever spoke to me.

That night as I sat in my tent, a lieutenant told me that one of our captains was killed, and on my mentioning their names he said it was Dickey. I could not believe it, but the next morning the news was confirmed.

It was too true. Not ten minutes after I left, one of those occasional bullets had crashed through his brain. He lived, or breathed rather, for forty-eight hours after, but I could not go to see him.

By and by they brought him to me—all that was left of my friend lay before me on a stretcher in an ambulance.

Just after the battle of Olustee he had given me the address of his mother (he had no father) and his sister, and I had given him your address and my father's, and we promised each other that if anything occurred, (we expressed it in that way with the natural dread of speaking of death) that if anything occurred to one, and the other was spared he should write to our friends the sad news. The sad fulfillment of the promise was mine, and I took his body to the embalmer's and had it prepared and sent to his friends, as I knew he would have done for me under like circumstances. It was all I could do, and now I sit and gaze on his picture and think of all his noble, manly, generous qualities and I know how his mother and his sister must mourn for him, but our grief can never return him to us....

Well, dear sister, I send you my diary, such as it is. There will be much of it that you cannot understand and much that would not interest you if you could. There are many references to persons who are strange to you, and but very little of any part will pay you for the reading. To me, I have a fancy that it will be very interesting in after years. It will recall to me scenes and incidents that without it I should have forgotten. I have kept it in a careless, desultory manner, and with no expectation that it would interest any but myself. Indeed a diary would be more appropriately named an "*I*-ary," for there is little else but "I" in it. Still, if you find any amusement or enjoyment in it, it will be an additional source of pleasure to me. I ask you to keep it for me, and perhaps at some future time we may look it over together and pass a pleasant hour in so doing.

Source: [OWN]

❧

CONVERTING THE YANKEES: *"Within the past two weeks I have preached 10 times"*

Reverend H. Brown
Richmond, Virginia
January 27, 1865

To Miss Elen Martin

My dear Friend—

Yours of the 24th with $150, enclosed, was received today, and the money disposed of according to directions. The Tracts have been procured and will be forwarded by the first opportunity. I am very glad of the prospect of a box, and hope there may be an opportunity to send it. Such acts of kindness not only add greatly to my comfort, but effect me very sensibly. Although we should never be distrustful of the good providence of our Heavenly Father, yet what shall we eat, and wherewithal shall we be clothed, must, while we live, occasion anxiety and care. I get along much better in the eating than heretofore. Our bread is quite passable—much better than at any time since I have been connected with the army. It is baked by Yankee prisoners, who prefer to do it, to remaining in confinement, or to going home to be sent back to the army. I eat by myself in my room, bread, and occasionally meat is brought. The beef is so poor however that I rarely eat it; but the bread, with such additions as I make to it, leaves me no ground of complaint. Under these circumstances you can see that a box from friends is likely to be valued highly. I am glad to be able to say that at this time, the number of sick soldiers, in and around this city, is very small. In this camp the number at the beginning of the present month was about 65. It is now about 35. To these I endeavor to minister in holy things in various ways, and have reason to believe that my labors are not in vain. Within a few days past, two I trust, have passed from death unto life. A few weeks ago one died in about as happy a frame of mind as I ever knew.

On last Saturday, that bitter day of rain and ice, 570 paroled prisoners came into camp. Soon follows, wet and cold, (two of them with nothing that resembled the name of shoes or stockings,) how it touched me to see them. Nearly all however have since been paid, and clothed, and furloughed, and have gone home. Except these, we have had but few in this camp for some time. Not having much to do in my own charge I often go abroad. Within the past two weeks I have preached 10 times. Of these, discourses, two were preached to the Yankee deserters, who have come over to us under order 65. Near me, and indeed all around the city, is a hive of breast works, all along which pickets are stationed. Several miles of these I visit once a week with religious newspapers and Tracts I have preached also in each of the hospitals attached to the Libby prison. All this, in addition to my daily duties in this camp and hospitals does not leave me entirely unemployed.

I have preached twice recently to our own people…On each of these occasions most of those who were not in close confinement attended and were orderly. The Yankee deserters, with some exceptions attended, and those who did attend behaved very well. On each occasion I noticed several in tears. At the close of service some of them introduced themselves, and others gathered round for a chat. They gave me many thanks for coming, and many requests to repeat my visits. Of course I said nothing about the war but in a very general way. Those to whom I preached have, as I understand, all left for their own land, and as many more are in their places.

In the hospitals attached to the Libby prison, some were attentive, and some were not. One sobbed through nearly half the Sermon, but quite a number seemed to say in their countenances, "Well, this is an effort to heap coals of fire on our heads for the devilment we have done in Virginia."

On the whole, as long as I have as much as I can do among our own people I will preach to them "Let the children first be fine"; after that I, as far as possible, "preach the Gospel to every creature." It can do the Yankees no harm, and may do them good. The tendency of a little kindness to them in their distress may be to soften their feelings.

For war news I must refer you to the newspapers. Our President after having well nigh ruined the country, has evidently largely laid aside his annoying self conceit in his own abilities, and his mulishness. This, and the appointment of a Commander in chief, has wonderfully revived the spirits of the people. Col. Ould told an acquaintance of mine two days ago that he now entertains strong hopes of a speedy general exchange of prisoners. The 570 who came last Saturday were in better flight than any I have seen. We have no late letter from my son. Remember me very kindly to your Sister, and to your brother & family.

Yours very Sincerely

P.S. There is no doubt of a great effort for peace on both sides at this time. [Vice President of the Confederacy Alexander H.] Stephens, [Robert M. T.] Hunter, and Judge [John A.] Campbell have gone to Washington for that object.

General-in-Chief Robert E. Lee, C.S.A.
Headquarters, Confederate States Armies
March 2, 1865

To Lieutenant General Ulysses S. Grant, U.S.A.

Commanding U. S. Armies: General:

   Lieutenant-General Longstreet has informed me that in a recent conversation between himself and Major-General Ord as to the possibility of arriving at a satisfactory adjustment of the present unhappy difficulties by means of a military convention, General Ord stated that if I desired to have an interview with you on the subject you would not decline, provided I had authority to act. Sincerely desiring to leave nothing untried which may put an end to the calamities of war, I propose to meet you at such convenient time and place as you may designate, with the hope that upon an interchange of views it may be found practicable to submit the subjects of controversy between the belligerents to a convention of the kind mentioned. In such event I am authorized to do whatever the result of the proposed interview may render necessary or advisable. Should you accede to this proposition I would suggest that, if agreeable to you, we meet at the place selected by Generals Ord and Longstreet for their interview at 11 a.m. on Monday next.

                    Very respectfully, your obedient servant
                    R. E. LEE,
                    General

Lieutenant General Grant could not accede to any talks that did not call for Lee's army's surrender.

Source: [WOR]

⚬

Lieutenant General Ulysses S. Grant, U.S.A.

Appomattox Court House
Head Quarters Armies of the United States
Appomattox Court House, Virginia
April 9, 1865

To General R. E. Lee, Commanding C.S.A.

General,—

In accordance with the substance of my letter to you of the 8th instant, I propose to receive the surrender of the Army of Northern Virginia on the following terms, to wit: Rolls of all the officers and men to be made in duplicate, one copy to be given to an officer to be designated by me, the other to be retained by such officer or officers as you may designate. The officers to give their individual paroles not to take up arms against the Government of the United States until properly exchanged; and each company or regimental commander sign a like parole for the men of their commands. The arms, artillery, and public property to be parked and stacked, and turned over to the officers appointed by me to receive them. This will not embrace the side-arms of the officers, nor their private horses or baggage. This done, each officer and man will be allowed to return to his home, not to be disturbed by U.S. authority so long as they observe their paroles and the laws in force where they may reside.

U.S. GRANT
Lieutenant-General

Grant handed this letter to Lee at Appomattox Court House, which Lee, in a note, accepted.

$\sim$

Edwin Marsh, U.S.A.
15th New York Cavalry, General Custer's Division
Virginia, Camp in a Field
April 14, 1865

To His Aunt Julia

Dear Aunt—

We have had so much fighting to do that we have not had time for anything else but sleeping, eating, and marching; all of which we did in the latest and most approved style. The Third Division of Cavalry, under command of General Sheridan and General Custer, started from Petersburg and marched to the right of the line and commenced the battle. General Custer drove the rebels from their position; and when we got them started we kept them going, but at night the rebels made a stand, and then we would flank them and drive them out, capture some prisoners, a battle-flag, or a battery, and then chase them again. But of all the battles that ever I was in, the fight of Harper's Farms was a little the hottest.

Our regiment was in advance. General Custer rode up, with his band playing "Hail Columbia," "Star Spangled Banner," and "Rally Round the Flag, Boys," and then the bugle sounded the charge. Away we went, with our sabres swinging at our wrists, ready to grasp at a moment's warning, and our carbines at an advance, ready for use. We had not gone more than forty rods, when the rebels opened fire upon us from three points, with grape and canister, solid shot, and shell, and musketry. We charged up to the face of the rebel batteries, under their fire; but we had to retreat. In the second charge, however, we captured their batteries and a number of prisoners.

The name of Sheridan will live always in the memory of the American people! It was glorious to see him seize the battle-flag, and ride to that part of the line where the fire was hottest and the fight the hardest. But the most glorious part of it all was Lee's surrender!

Sounding the Charge

General Custer was riding at the head of our regiment when the flag of truce came out, but the general did not wish to halt—he wished to whip them completely; but we had to stop and wait the arrival of the flag of truce, and listen to the message from Lee. General Custer's reply was, "Tell your commander we are on his front, his flank, and rear. Our only conditions are his surrender." This message was sent at ten o'clock Sunday morning, April 9th, and Lee surrendered at 4 o'clock p.m.

It was, indeed, a glorious sight to see the rebels lay down their arms. I intended to send you some relic from the scene where the papers of capitulation were signed, but I have been ill and could not. We fired one hundred guns today, in honor of our flag being raised again over Sumter.

Source: [SL]

THE ASSASSINATION OF ABRAHAM LINCOLN: *"We are all dumb with grief"*

Caroline C. Woolsey
New York City
Saturday Morning, April 15, 1865

To Her Sister, Eliza Woolsey Howland

Dear Eliza:

What can one do? We are all dumb with grief. The extra has just been cried giving the awful moment of his death. What a moment for America! When you think of his unvarying kindness toward those very men who now rejoice,—how his whole career has been one of goodness and mercy, and now at the very first beginning of reward, it is too hard to bear. The papers were brought up while we were in bed this morning. You have hardly heard it now. I suppose you will not come down today, but you must on Monday. Charley is in Washington, in rooms with General Williams, on 15th Street. New York seems dead, the streets are quiet and the flags all covered with black crape—even the "extra" boys subdue their voices. Work is suspended, and Wall Street is thronged with silent men.

Do come down; we ought to be together in these awful times.

Eliza Woolsey Howland and another sister served as nurses in the war and were from New York City.

Source: Georgeanna Muirson (Woolsey) Bacon and Eliza Woolsey Howland. *Letters of a Family During the War for the Union, 1861–1865.* New Haven: Tuttle, Morehouse and Taylor, 1899. [LF]

∾

Sarah E. Andrews
Hudson, Wisconsin
April 16, 1865

To James A. Andrews

Dear Brother Jimmie,

A week ago today I wrote you that it was a day of rejoicing over victories achieved. Today that joy is turned to sorrow. Last night the news reached us that Lincoln had been assassinated.

Today in church while they were singing the second time someone handed Mr. Keeley a paper announcing the death of Lincoln and Seward. It was the first the congregation had heard of their death. All had hoped they might live. I don't think there was a dry eye in the church when he read it. His feelings so overcame him he asked to be excused from preaching this morning. After a short prayer the congregation were dismissed. It has cast a gloom over the entire north. All have felt the shock. I had hoped our difficulties were about to be settled, but now hope has almost died. When, yes, when will this war cease? God only knows. I hope our Vice President will be competent to fill the vacancy. He will be in favor of hanging the traitors. I have thought it would be hardly right to do so; but I think I have changed my mind somewhat within the last twenty four hours.

For once in a life time we were ready for church in the morning long before it was time. I got ready and sat down and commenced a letter to Charlie while waiting for the minute hand of the clock to point at half past ten. Emory has just been in. He came over after Ada. She has been over since Thursday.

She and Lib went to Catholic church today. It is Easter Sunday. Nellie [Chambers] is going to commence attending school tomorrow. She is very much pleased. She will probably be quite an accomplished young lady when you come home. She is going to that Mrs. Watson that lives up near Mr. Humphreys. She sends her love to you.

I am not in a writing mood today, so I hope you will excuse a partly-filled sheet. Write soon and often to your much attached sister,

SARAH E. ANDREWS

[P.S.] Mother thinks if you have not got your socks and wrapper you had better send to Nashville and if they are there have them sent to you.

James A. Andrews was serving in Company A, 44th Regiment Wisconsin Volunteer Infantry.

Source: http://www.factasy.com/civil_war/book/export/html/665 [FAC] (See also: *Postmarked Hudson: The Letters of Sarah A. Andrews to Her Brother, James A. Andrews, 1864–65.* Compiled and Edited by Willis Harry Miller. Hudson, Wisconsin: Star Observer Publishing Company, 1955. James A. Andrews and John Comstock Papers, 1837–1946. Also: Wisconsin Historical Society Archives.)

Sources

Anecdotes, Poetry, and Incidents of the War: North and South: 1860–1865. Frank Moore, editor. New York, 1866. [API]

Georgeanna Muirson (Woolsey) Bacon and Eliza Woolsey Howland. *Letters of a Family During the War for the Union, 1861–1865.* New Haven: Tuttle, Morehouse and Taylor, 1899. [LF]

Benjamin F. Butler. *Private and Official Correspondence of Gen. Benjamin F. Butler.* Volume 2. Edited by Benjamin Franklin Butler, Jessie Ames Marshall. Norwood, Massachusetts: Plimpton Press, 1917. [BFB]

Civil War Home: (Dick Weeks. Shotgun's Home of the American Civil War.) http://www.civilwarhome.com/newtonletter.htm [CWH]

A Cycle of Adams Letters, 1861-1865. Volumes 1-2. Edited by Worthington Chauncey Ford. Boston: Houghton Mifflin, 1920. [CAL-1, CAL-2]

Electronic Text Center, University of Virginia Library. [ETC]

factasy.com/civil_war/book/export/html/665 [FAC] (See also: *Postmarked Hudson: The Letters of Sarah A. Andrews to Her Brother, James A. Andrews, 1864–65.* Compiled and Edited by Willis Harry Miller. Hudson, Wisconsin: Star Observer Publishing Company, 1955. James A. Andrews and John Comstock Papers, 1837–1946. Also: Wisconsin Historical Society Archives.)

Ulysses S. Grant. *Letters of Ulysses S. Grant to His Father and His Youngest Sister, 1857–78.* Edited by Jesse Grant Cramer. New York: G. P. Putnam's Sons, 1912. [USG]

P. A. Hanaford. *The Young Captain: A Memorial of Capt. Richard C. Derby.* Boston: Degen, Estes, and Company, 1865. [YC]

Mary Anna Jackson. *Memoirs of Stonewall Jackson.* Louisville, Kentucky: Prentice Press, 1895. [MSJ]

John William Jones. *Christ in Camp: Or Religion in Lee's Army*. Richmond: B. F. Johnson and Company, 1887. [JWJ]

Robert E. Lee. *Recollections and Letters of General Robert E. Lee, Volume 3.* Edited by his son, Robert Edward Lee. New York: Doubleday, Page and Company, 1904. [REL]

Abraham Lincoln. *Abraham Lincoln: His Speeches and Writings.* Edited by Roy P. Basler. Cleveland: The World Publishing Company, 1946. [AL]

Love Letters of the Civil War. Digital Library and Archives, University Libraries, Virginia Polytechnic Institute and State University. http://spec.lib.vt.edu/cwlove/jcmorris.html [LL]

George C. McClellan. *McClellan's Own Story: The War for the Union, the Soldiers Who Fought, the Civilians Who Directed It and His Relations to It and to Them.* New York: Charles L. Webster & Company, 1887. [MOS]

George B. McClellan. *Civil War Papers of George B. McClellan.* Edited by Stephen W. Sears. New York: Ticknor and Fields, 1989. [GBM]

Randolph Harrison McKim. *A Soldier's Recollections: Leaves from the Diary of a Young Confederate.* New York: Longmans, Green and Company, 1921. [ASR]

John Singleton Mosby. *The Memoirs of Colonel John S. Mosby.* Boston: Little, Brown and Company, 1917. [JSM]

Oliver Willcox Norton. *Army Letters, 1861–1865: Being Extracts from Private Letters to Relatives.* Chicago, 1903. [OWN]

The William Dorsey Pender Papers, #1059, Southern Historical Collection, The Wilson Library, University of North Carolina at Chapel Hill. See also William W. Hassler's *The General to His Lady: The Civil War Letters of William Dorsey Pender to Fanny Pender.* Chapel Hill: The University of North Carolina Press, 1965. [WDP]

George E. Pickett. *The Heart of a Soldier: As Revealed in the Intimate Letters of George E. Pickett C. S. A.* New York: Seth Moyle, 1913. [GEP]

The Rebellion Record: A Diary of American Events, with Documents, Narratives, Illustrative Incidents, Poetry, Etc. Volume 7. Frank Moore, editor. New-York: D. Van Nostrand, 1864. [RR7]

Soldiers' Letters from Camp, Battlefield, and Prison. Edited by Lydia Minturn Post. New York: Bunce and Huntington, Publishers, 1865. [SL] (This is an outstanding collection but chaotically organized.)

Soldierstudies.org [SS]

Emily Bliss Thacher Souder. *Leaves from the Battle-field*. Philadelphia: Caxton Press of C. Sherman & Co, 1864. [EBTS]

William Jewett Tenney. *The Military and Naval History of the Rebellion in the United States*. New York: D. Appleton and Company, 1866. [WJT]

The Valley of the Shadow Personal Papers. Electronic Text Center, the University of Virginia Library. Virginia Center for Digital History. Henry H. and Mary E. A. Dedrick Letters. The War Years. http://valley.lib.virginia.edu/VoS/personalpapers/documents/augusta/p2dedrickletters.html [VS]

The War of the Rebellion: A Compilation of the Official Records of the Union and Confederate Armies. United States War Department. Washington, D.C.: Government Printing Office, 1899. [WOR]

Walt Whitman. *The Wound Dresser: A Series of Letters Written from the Hospitals in Washington During the War of the Rebellion*. Edited by Richard Maurice Bucke. Boston: Small, Maynard and Company, 1898.

The Wisconsin Magazine of History, Vol. 4, 1920–21. Publications of the State Historical Society of Wisconsin. Edited by Milo M. Quaife. [WMH]